Aging
is
an
Attitude

Cecil Murphey

Aging is an Attitude

**Positive Ways to
Look at Getting Older**

LIVING
INK
BOOKS
Writing Worth Reading

Contents

CONTENTS

Acknowledgments

S pecial thanks to Shirley and David. As they read about themselves, once again, they can see how special they are in my life. I'm grateful to my agent Deidre Knight who believed in this book and to Dan Penwell who was the first editor to see the book, like it, and make an offer. Elaine Wright Colvin's fingerprints are on the concept of this book, and I want to thank her.

In writing this book, I depended on the accumulated wisdom of many. I've tried to list all their names here and the things they shared with me. Thank you to each of you: Leonard and Marilyn Auton, Marlene Bagnull, Phil Barnhart, Patrick Borders, Maggie Campbell, Robert Carpenter, Stan Cottrell, Jon Drury, Burt Dumont, Lannie Dumont, Anne Dunnivin, Jimmy Durran, Eva Marie Everson, Bud Ferguson, Pat Fields, Betty Freeman, Mark Hammell, Sr., Cliff Harris, Jana Heirent, Marion Hill, Bernie Kida, James Kern, Samantha Landy, Yvonne Lehman, Sr., Ellen List, Marty Nelson, Roger Palms, Patti Patterson, Dr. William Patterson, Chuck Pekios, Jeff Peterson-Davis, Don Renner, Karen Rosen, Ralph Simmons, Wiley Sloan, David Talbott, James Tate, Jeff Turner, Susan Wales, Chuck White, and JoAnn Wray.

Introduction: Enjoying a New Place

W hat is the most positive thing you can say about getting older?" I began to ask that question because I got tired of groaning and moaning from people who obviously weren't enjoying their lives.

This book came into focus while I was teaching at the Mount Hermon Christian Writers' Conference in California. Between sessions, I approached individuals who were clearly middle-aged and older. I asked one question: "For you, what is the most positive thing you can say about getting older?"

While they pondered, I told them I planned to write a book on the topic and if I used their answers, I'd quote them and list their names. (A few who answered chose not to have their names used. In that case, I have changed a few details and shown this with an asterisk.) I have asked this question to more than a hundred individuals, most of them in person, but some by e-mail.

One of the first persons to e-mail me in response was Mark Hammell, Sr. He wrote: "After years of feeling guilty about thinking of myself as old or being afraid of getting older, pretending that I hadn't changed and everything was the same, I'm free. I can now say I'm enjoying a new place. I no longer have to compete with the youth market or live up

> "I'm getting more and more comfortable being me, and the more I understand who I am, the more I like myself."

to others' expectations. I'm setting my own standards for myself and enjoying my life much more. I learned to play tennis at age fifty-four and started classes in square dancing. To my surprise, I enjoy these activities." Mark is now in his sixties.

Mark isn't the only person with a positive, upbeat attitude. He was only the first to respond.

One of my favorite answers came from Maggie Campbell who said, "I'm getting more and more comfortable being me, and the more I understand who I am, the more I like myself."

Many helped me think of aspects about aging that hadn't occurred to me. Their openness enabled me to examine my own attitudes. I began to see getting older as a time of continued growth and not as one of decline. I slowly learned to regard aging as *my time* of continued growth.

> We can't choose to age—God has made that choice for us—but we can choose how to respond to the process.

I've struggled over aging a great deal. My wife Shirley glided into becoming a senior citizen—or at least that's my perception of how well she's handled it. My best friend Dave Morgan and I have spent a lot of time discussing this topic. Although Dave is ten years my junior, he's taught me a lot about accepting yourself as an emerging older person.

Here's the conclusion I reached in talking to baby boomers and seniors: We can't choose to age—God has made that choice for us—but we can choose how to respond to the process. A major factor in successful aging is to embrace the advantages of growing older.

The people in this book have chosen to see life as an ongoing adventure. They are proving that the later years can be as challenging and exciting as the earlier ones. In fact, some would say these years are even better.

Facing the Fear

Getting older used to scare me—and I suspect I'm not alone. Researching and writing this book has eased some of that fear, but a deep, underlying dread still sneaks up on me occasionally. Just when I think I've gotten it all figured out, fear of getting older creeps in and the battle goes on again.

On the positive side, my life is getting easier and I'm enjoying myself more. I don't have kids to put through school or orthodontic bills staring me in the face, and I no longer wonder if we can afford dinner at an expensive restaurant. My wife and I have numerous options on how we spend our money and what we do with our free time. I still work full-time as a writer, but I can choose my projects and not worry if I can survive financially.

Once in a while, however, I peer ahead and recognize that the end of my life is closer than the beginning. Reality rushes in to remind me that I am aging, and that's when fear tries to strangle my present enjoyment.

Why this dread of getting older? I can immediately mention three reasons. The first is because of images tucked deeply inside my head. I hold several vivid memories of and about seniors that disturb me; I worry that I might end up like them. If so, I want to delay the aging as long as possible.

Here are four pictures that presented a negative view and have stayed with me.

1. I visited a senior citizens' center and overheard a group of gray and bald heads describe their latest remedy for constipation—their voices sounded as excited as if they enthused over a new diet.

2. One evening, an elderly couple sat across from me in the food court at Atlanta's Lenox Mall. They commented on girls wearing skirts that barely covered their thighs and boys with pants slung so low that they looked as if they might fall off. The woman raised her eyebrows and I heard her say, "When we were young . . ." and later, she started a sentence with, "In the old days . . ."

3. At age thirty-three, *Doug told me about talking with his sponsor at Alcoholics Anonymous. He didn't like the man and grumbled about the constant advice he had to listen to. "Anyway, he's sixty years old," Doug said. "What does he know about life today?"

At the time I had just turned sixty-two.

4. When a well-known literary agent died, a writer-friend said, "She was an old woman." She then used words such as "tottering," "fragile," and "ancient." A few days later I learned

the woman died at age seventy-one. She was older than I was at that time—*older by one year.*

That's the first reason—others' perceptions about growing older. I hate the idea of being judged as elderly, senile, or incapacitated based strictly by dates on the calendar.

Here's a second reason. Although those images are prejudicial enough, fear clutches at me most powerfully when I look at individuals whose minds have frozen. They stopped thinking new thoughts and avoided exploring different ideas. It's as if they died at age forty-five but won't have the funeral until they're seventy-five.

> I hate the idea of being judged as elderly, senile, or incapacitated based strictly by dates on the calendar.

For instance, in the early 1990s, a seventy-two-year-old man discussed a theological book he wanted me to ghostwrite for him—and he held a position with which I disagreed. When I questioned his theology, he glared at me. "This is what I learned forty years ago. I'm not about to change now."

"Why not?" I asked.

"Then I would have to admit I was wrong."

Those words ended our discussion and we didn't do the book together. Although I never told him, I knew I didn't want to work with anyone who hadn't examined his theology in forty years. His thinking had fossilized a generation earlier.

The third reason for my fear, however, is the most difficult to write about: I don't like the idea of giving up, getting weaker, or depending on others to do things for me.

So there's no question about my age, I was born in 1933. Anyone can figure out how old I am. I also want to scream out, "Yes, but I'm healthy and alert." Other than the loss of a few teeth (military service-related), I have all my original parts and they all work well. I run twenty-four miles a week and walk twelve. I take no medication, and my weight rests comfortably in the low–normal range.

Oops, there I go! As I finished writing the above, I realized I was defending myself against appearing old and pushing away the perception of me as an old man. I don't want anyone to think of me as forty-five, but I don't like looking at facing the end.

Now that I've laid out my fears about aging, I confess that every morning my mirror reminds me that my wrinkles weren't there when I was twenty and the gray hairs hadn't appeared by the time I was thirty. I *am* getting older. To live honestly and authentically, I need to face the reality of aging just as I did puberty and teenaged angst.

> To live authentically, I need to face the reality of aging just as I did puberty and teenaged angst.

As I've begun to analyze my anxieties, I admit that most of them have centered on aging as a sliding-rapidly-down-the-slope-to-the-end experience. My observations and accepted prejudices make me sound as if I'm a prisoner on death row, visibly confined, and awaiting the eventual day of execution. That image sounds extreme and irrational, and yet that's the kind of hold fear about aging has on many of us over fifty. Mine wasn't that extreme, but it was there.

Now I want to make it clear what this book is *not* about. It is not about denying aging. It is not about overcoming barriers to encourage us to try to remake ourselves into youthful figures (a form of denial). It is not about accepting senility with a smile or physical disability with a shrug and saying, "Well, after all, I'm nearly eighty." It's not about how to look, act, or feel ten years younger.

> I want to enjoy the third phase of my life and share the benefits with others.

My purpose in writing is quite simple: I want to enjoy the third phase of my life and share the benefits with others. I also want to share the positive insights of others as they view themselves stepping ahead in the aging process.

I survived childhood and merged into adulthood. As I've gone through the various stages of adult life, I've enjoyed my life immensely. Now that I face this final segment, I don't want to slink back, deny, or struggle. I want this to be a natural progress in my search for self-understanding and a closer relationship with God. As I share my discoveries and those of the people I've interviewed, I believe we can encourage others to sign up for life's final adventure.

The best way I can describe this phase is by remembering that when I was a child, I could hardly wait to be old enough to go to school. Then I yearned to be an adolescent and anticipated the day when I could call myself a teenager. After that I wanted to drive a car, vote, and get married. I raced and stumbled onward, yet always excited about the path that lay before me. There was always another mountain to climb.

Today, I know I still have at least one major mountain ahead. I want to go forward with boldness and honesty. If I stopped racing ahead now, I'd be turning against the very principles by which I have lived. I've decided to keep moving forward. I've chosen to run and play and dance into the future instead of being dragged into it.

> I've chosen to run and play and dance into the future instead of being dragged into it.

That's where positive aging begins for me. It's an excitement about the as-yet-unexperienced joys that are right around the next bend in the road. If all the other stages have been worth living for, why wouldn't this be the best yet?

Embracing Age

L ife can continue to be an adventure and I've enlisted as a joyous volunteer. The last mountains we climb can excite and challenge us as much as any of the others we've faced. Because we've experienced many battles in life, we have accumulated the resources to equip us for life's final chapter. Because we have to put more effort and concentration on the upward climb, maybe we can enjoy the vista of accomplishment far more.

At the same time, honesty forces me to admit that I'm moving into what people refer to as the "declining years." If they mean decreased energy and creaking bodies, they're right. Yet God compensates for the physical decline by increasing the mental prowess and the appreciation of the journey we've already traveled.

Instead of always focusing on where we're going, we can smile and enjoy where we've been and—even more—relish the scenery of where we are now.

I'm learning to acknowledge the joyful compensations and to explore a variety of possibilities of happier living.

> God compensates for the physical decline by increasing the mental prowess and the appreciation of the journey we've already traveled.

As I've already said, I can't choose to age—God made that decision for me; however, I *can* choose how to respond to aging. I can trudge mournfully downhill, put an out-of-business sign on my mind, curse the deterioration of my body, and grumble at the injustices of life. I can choose to fight the progressive decline— and that battle can only go on for a short time anyway. Even if I tried to hide my years with a facelift, hair coloring, and a red, five-speed sports car, inside I'd still know I wasn't a Beach Boy, and no one would mistake me for thirty-five again.

So how have I dealt with aging?

First, I began by choosing a position I call acceptance. I wanted to admit to myself—with a smile on my face—that I'm getting older. On a regular basis I reminded myself of that fact. I still run four times a week, but I have learned to say, "I don't have to do eight-minute miles." My speed has slowed to about ten minutes a mile. Some mornings, I walk part of the way. I decided I wanted to be thankful that God had given me good health so I can exercise regularly. Each morning before I head down the street in my running shoes,

I silently thank God that I can still run and enjoy it—and enjoy every part of my life.

That's acceptance.

But that wasn't enough.

More recently, I selected a word that feels more comfortable. I chose to *embrace* aging. To embrace the aging process means not only to accept myself *as I am* and to look joyfully ahead, but the term also means to delight in the advantages of growing older.

Second, I focused on aging as a positive factor in my life. If God planned for us to get older, why should I argue and call this phase of life negative? Is it possible, I asked myself, that God intended the last years to be the best? Instead of slinking into oblivion, could the divine plan encourage us to sing the hymns of triumph all the way to the grave? Can it be that God wants us to enjoy our final part of the journey as much as we did the first two parts? Perhaps enjoy it even more?

> I chose to *embrace* aging. To embrace the aging process means not only to accept myself *as I am* and to look joyfully ahead, but the term also means to delight in the advantages of growing older.

I decided the answer was a resounding yes. My task was to learn to live by embracing this final, triumphant phase of my life.

As I pondered many self-questions, I realized I had truly begun to embrace the process. I couldn't have faced these issues if I lived in denial or remained unwilling to admit what is going on inside me. Not only does honesty force me to admit that I'm moving into the final years, I am also learning to acknowledge the joyful compensations and to explore a variety of possibilities that will make my life even more meaningful.

I'm not alone in this choice. Many others have blazed a trail for us to follow. No matter what our chronological age, we're getting older. If we can courageously affirm our aging and enjoy the privileges of this stage in life, we'll help make the world a happier place. I believe that each of us influences others every day and in every situation. Why not make that a positive factor? Better still, we can be happier and more contented. Best of all, we can pause and thank our all-loving God for such wisdom for the whole gamut of human creation and for allowing us to live long enough to enjoy the final phase of growth.

This makes me think of the New Testament story of Jesus and his mother going to a wedding. In that familiar story, the wine ran out and Jesus turned six large pots of water into wine. The best part of the story wasn't the miracle, but that Jesus had provided wine of a superior quality.

"The master of the banquet . . . said, 'Everyone brings out the choice wine first and then the cheaper wine after the guests have had too much to drink; but you have saved the best till now' " (John 2:9–10 NIV).

What would it be if we truly considered the last years the best? What if we thought of all the younger days and years as preparation to enjoy the best years?

I love the comment made by Nobel Prize winner Pearl S. Buck: "Would I wish to be 'young' again? No, for I have learned too much to wish to lose it. It would be like failing to pass a grade in school. I have reached an honorable position in life, because I am old and no longer young. I am a far more valuable person today than I was 50 years ago, or 40 years ago, or 30, 20, or even 10. I HAVE LEARNED SO MUCH SINCE I WAS 70! . . . This, I suppose is because I have perfected my techniques, so that I no longer waste time in learning how to do what I have to do."[1]

That's positive aging.

I suspect God smiled and might even have said, "You have the right answer."

An Older Person?

I want to share three illustrations with you, all of them true and all of them forcing individuals to face stark realities.

1. "Let those old women get through," one of the teens said and smiled at two women. Katherine, aged fifty-four, shocked to hear the girl's words, stared at her fifty-two-year-old friend. "Guess that's us," she said and plastered a smile on her face.

"Are we really old?" whispered Katherine's friend. "Or are they so young they don't know the difference?"

Katherine's sense of humor had returned by then and she said, "Maybe we're so old, *we* don't know the difference."

2. "I went to my fortieth high school reunion," *Chuck told his son. "Everyone there was so old. Two former classmates came in wheelchairs and one former

football player was almost blind." He sighed and shook his head. "So old. All of them so old."

"What do you think you are?" his son asked.

"Well, I—I guess I'm the same age, but I'm not—not—" Then he stared in bewilderment. "I guess I—I thought I was all right and maybe a little younger."

3. "I told him there's an older man I wanted him to meet." Those were the words of my friend, ultramarathon runner Stan Cottrell, as he related a phone conversation with a business associate. He referred to me as the older man. I nodded and tried to listen to the reasons he wanted us to get together. I didn't hear much of the explanation because one phrase kept pushing at me. Stan had referred to me as "an older man."

> "A person is always startled when he hears himself seriously called an old man for the first time."—Oliver Wendell Holmes

Forty-one-year-old Stan was talking about *me.*

Me? An older man?

I said nothing to Stan, who didn't realize the effect of that phrase on me, but as I drove home, I kept thinking of those three words: *an older man.* I was fifty-one years old at the time. Was that old? Was that when the separation began between young, middle-aged, and elderly?

It reminds me of a comment made by Oliver Wendell Holmes: "A person is always startled when he hears himself seriously called an old man for the first time." Yes, Stan's words had startled me.

Until that moment, I had considered myself comfortably middle-aged. Our three kids were grown, married, and we had grandchildren. But "an older man"?

For many of us, there's an implied something-is-wrong-with-me-if-I'm-an-older-person mindset. Perhaps that's why many work hard to look younger. Maybe what we need is to accept our age as an achievement. We've made it. We've survived the hard years of growing up. Now we're ready to enjoy the golden years.

Not everyone has those traumatic moments of being suddenly part of the older generation. I remember when Jim Pinson hit forty and depression at the same time. "I feel old," he said.

I had little sympathy for his statement. Maybe it was because I then was in my thirties and hadn't yet faced the reality of mounting years and the body wearing down.

Yes, I've been forced to admit, I am an older man. Like every other living person on this planet, I am getting older. For me, it took a drastic mind shift to place myself in that older-man category.

> In accepting the label of "an older person," I realized that my concern really had little to do with actually getting older.

In accepting the label of "an older person," I realized that my concern really had little to do with actually getting older. It had to do with facing the reality that I was no longer among the "*now* generation"— the current crop of twenty-to-thirty-year-olds who decide the fashion trends, the movies, and the latest styles of music.

It wasn't my aging that bothered me, but I struggled with what I considered the perception of other people—that is, the perception of younger people. Too often the attitude I encounter says, "If young is good then old must be bad; if children represent tomorrow, then older people must stand for yesterday."

Or maybe I reflected my own myopic viewpoint of older people. I vividly remembered two older couples in the first church I joined. They had hit fifty and they looked ancient to me at age twenty-two. But even more serious, they had stopped growing. Their attitudes had frozen years earlier, and they tried to push us to live by the standards they had grown up with.

Is that who I am? I asked myself. Is that what it means to be an older person? Yes, I *was* one of them.

At first, I felt a wave of depression come over me. Then I paused to reflect. I remember hearing older people kidding and saying, "Getting old is better than the alternative." Now I understood what they meant. They weren't clutching at life, but they were trying to say—I hope—that they were still on this earth and still enjoying being alive.

I also realized something else: I belong to God. When I was in my early twenties I surrendered my life to Jesus Christ. Little did I understand that's when the journey of my life actually started. At least, it was the start of my true, spiritual life. As I've continued to live, Jesus Christ has walked with me through all those years.

As I continued to ponder the aging process, I remembered Paul's admonition to Timothy, "Don't let anyone think less of you because you are young. Be an example to all believers in what you teach, in the way you live, in your love, your faith, and your purity" (1 Tim. 4:12 NLT). Apparently, older believers belittled Timothy because he was younger, and Paul urged him to stand up for himself.

Then I smiled. Maybe that's the way it always is. No matter what our age, we sense we're discriminated against. Before we're legally called adults, we feel pushed aside and unimportant, because we're only kids. When we're called senior citizens, we feel as if we've lost our value. If we're middle-aged, we're too old to remember the dating problems. If we're in our twenties, our empty-nest friends and those who've become grandparents smile indulgently as if to say, "Your turn will come."

Is it possible that no matter what age we are, someone always thinks it's the wrong age? And worse—*we* accept such judgments as valid! Maybe there is truly no "right" age. Or maybe we've looked at it wrong. Maybe the right age is where we are now. Can it be that no matter how many wrinkles we have, or even if the pimples haven't yet appeared on our cheeks, it doesn't make any difference to God?

> Is it possible that no matter what age we are, someone always thinks it's the wrong age? And worse—*we* accept such judgments as valid!

I'm at the right age *now*. I've always been at the right age. I'm now among the older generation. Yes, I'm an older person, and God is as much with me now as when I first became a Christian. In fact, I'm more conscious of God's presence in my life than I've ever been before.

Isn't that positive aging?

Answering the Hard Question

Have you faithfully followed me since the day you were born again?"

God might ask the question that way—that is, when we first appear at the great heavenly throne. God knows everything, and yet in the Bible, God sometimes asks so that the hearers will reflect on their past behavior.

If God should ask it that way, I wonder how we would frame our answers. We'd remember wrongs, failings, shortcomings and, I assume, also remember that God forgave them. Yet even as we reflect, we'd probably do a hurried self-examination. We'd immediately think of every sin, large or small, that we had committed. Shame would sweep over us as we realized our foolish

> "Have you faithfully followed me since the day you were born again?" ...
>
> If God should ask it that way ... we'd probably do a hurried self-examination. We'd immediately think of every sin, large or small, that we had committed.

and selfish acts, our times of denial, and our moments of doubt.

Ultimately, we'd probably end up saying, "You know, Lord," and throw ourselves on God's mercy and grace. As we did so, we'd know that was the proper answer.

What if God next asked, "How faithfully did you take care of the temple while you were on earth?"

That's where most of us would have a difficult time. We might respond with, "What temple?" Or the question might make us think God referred to the holy temple in ancient Jerusalem.

As we stammered around, what if God's piercing eyes held ours and we heard, "How did you treat your bodies— *my* holy temple?"

Most of us would hang our heads in shame. A few would say, "I tried." Others might say, "No one ever taught much about *that.*"

Here's how the apostle Paul puts it: "So our aim is to please him always, whether we are here in this body or away from this body. For we must all stand before Christ to be judged. We will each receive whatever we deserve for the good or evil we have done in our bodies" (2 Cor. 5:9–10 NLT).

"Done in our bodies?" Of course, in that passage, Paul means more than the human temple we live in. He means our total lives and all our actions. But isn't it interesting that he uses the term *body*? It's also interesting that elsewhere Paul has other things to say about our treatment of the body. In fact, he refers to it as the Temple of God.

Who would deny that reality? Don't we evangelicals teach that God lives in temples not made with hands? That the Holy Spirit is within us? To put it a little clearer, here are three, straightforward biblical passages that are frequently overlooked or often ignored:

"Don't you realize that all of you together are the temple of God and that the spirit of God lives in you? God will bring ruin upon anyone who ruins this temple. For God's temple is holy, and you Christians are that temple" (1 Cor. 3:16–17 NLT).

"Or don't you know that your body is the temple of the Holy Spirit, who lives in you, and was given to you by God? You do not belong to yourself, for God bought you with a high price. So you must honor God with your body" (1 Cor. 6:19–20 NLT).

"And so, dear Christian friends, I plead with you to give your bodies to God. Let them be a living and holy sacrifice—the kind he will accept. When you think of what he has done for you, is that too much to ask?" (Rom. 12:1 NLT).

> Our bodies are sacred possessions of God. *They don't belong to us.*

In these verses we read a powerful message pleading with us to acknowledge that our bodies are sacred possessions of God. *They don't belong to us.* If we grasp that, then we readily understand Paul's admonition, "Whatever you eat or

19

> *Aging isn't the same as disease . . .* A properly maintained body shows the effects of aging gradually and leads its inhabitants gently into their seventies, eighties, and beyond. That's natural aging.

drink or whatever you do, you must do all for the glory of God" (1 Cor. 10:31 NLT).

When we have to stand before God, and if we are asked those questions, then what do we say?

If we're willing to ponder such a possibility, our response can help us in our aging journey. We're still alive, even if we're plagued with aches or dependent on medication. We can learn and change and begin to honor our holy temples. Some of us have mistreated our bodies by giving them too little sleep or by ignoring pain and warning symptoms. Others overate or ate too many unhealthy foods. We didn't exercise, even when we knew better. In short, most of us have not faithfully cared for God's temple.

I'm not writing to induce guilt; I *am* writing to get us to expand our thinking.

Who thinks much about health and physical fitness when they're ten years old? Few think much about caring for their bodies when they've reached their teens. In fact, I'm not sure where the awareness begins, but one day we're forced to acknowledge a reality—usually when something in our physical temple rebels. Then we face a startling revelation: Our bodies are not only getting older, but they're also wearing out.

Older people may have chronic, medicine-controlled health problems as they age, but they don't have to be limited by them. *Aging isn't the same as disease.* The sense of balance becomes less sure; the heart gradually loses its power, the metabolic rate slows, bones become brittle, skin thins out and becomes less elastic. The process doesn't happen to everyone at the same age or at the same rate. A properly maintained body will often show the effects of aging gradually and perhaps will lead its inhabitants gently into their seventies, eighties, and beyond. That's natural aging.

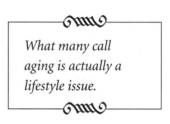

What many call aging is actually a lifestyle issue.

Aging differs from disease. A body subjected to continual stress, one that carries too much weight, that has been continually exposed to pollu-tants, has suffered years of poor nutrition, and has not been exercised regularly, will likely begin to show the effects of disease decades earlier.

In our book, *Live 10 Healthy Years Longer,*[2] Dr. Jan Kuzma and I point out the forty-year study, done by the National Institutes of Health and Loma Linda University, showing that many problems of old age aren't due to aging but to improper care of the body over a lifetime.

What many call aging is actually a lifestyle issue. Heart disease, osteoporosis, diabetes, and vascular disease are commonly classified as diseases of aging. That's true if the person is ninety, but when a fifty-year-old is so diagnosed, there's a good chance that the disease may be the result of a body wearing out prematurely. That reality hints strongly at the poor maintenance of God's temple. With optimal care, it's possible to grow old with energy and vigor and to live in the absence of disease.

I have a neighbor who is forty-nine years old. Two years

ago he suffered a heart attack. He survived and the doctor put him on a strict diet and an exercise program. "I'm going to change the way I live," he told me, and I encouraged him.

He reacted wonderfully for about a year. I saw him yesterday, the first time in maybe six months. He was mowing his lawn—perched on his riding mower—and I realized that although he had always been heavy, he must have gained at least forty pounds.

My purpose isn't to condemn. I suspect no one knows better than he does how badly he has ignored his physician's directives. He may be suffering from serious depression or a hundred other things I know nothing about.

> Sometimes we need reminding that "You do not belong to yourself. So you must honor God with your body."

Regardless, it's not too late for him to change. He's still alive. As long as breath flows through his body, there is place for repentance with our loving God.

Whether we're taught little or much, one of the realities of aging is that the temple of God ages as well. The level of care we give it has a great deal to do with the quality of those aging years. In the church, we've badly neglected talking about the holy temple, although that's beginning to change. Maybe we're finally realizing that we're responsible to care for God's temple.

Sometimes we need reminding that "You do not belong to yourself. So you must honor God with your body."

As we age and become aware of the slowing down and wear and tear on our bodies, it can enable us to pause and give thanks. It may also remind us of Paul's words that we don't belong to ourselves and that even our bodies are God's.

This theological thought also reminds me of how deeply God loves us. If our bodies are divine temples, they are God's dwelling places. God chose to reside in us and to honor us with his presence. Even if we haven't always honored that temple, it still reminds us of the special love God has for us. He is truly God within us.

> God chose to reside in us and to honor us with his presence.

This is also a reminder to us to pause and give thanks for these bodies that have served us well. We are still alive. We have endured. If we start—even now—to take better care of our holy temples, we can enjoy our lives even more.

Depending on Others

I finally figured out one major reason I don't like the concept of getting older: If I live long enough I will have to depend on someone else to take care of me. This is true of all of us.

Our culture, however, teaches exactly the opposite concept. We're people who stand on our feet. Do we need anyone else really? Haven't we been taught that we're strong and self-reliant? Don't we praise the up-by-the-bootstrap individuals and loudly applaud those who make life happen? We pride ourselves on our strong, individualized self-reliance.

Somewhere, someday, that situation changes—if we survive long enough. Instead of taking care of others and being the strong, independent types, others will have to take care of us. We may be forced to accept help, but we will have to have it.

It's not easy to make the shift. For many, that transition requires a strong mental and emotional adjustment. Some become dependent and resent every day of it.

It rarely happens that one day we're young, healthy, and vigorous, and the next day we're bedridden. Life gradually takes us down that pathway from running to being pushed in a wheelchair. We may not want to admit or face that the end of our independence is on the way, but that time will come.

> If I live long enough I will have to depend on someone else to take care of me.

As an example of this, one of the hardest things for older adults to do is to surrender their driver's licenses. As I wrote that sentence, I thought of the teens who eagerly await their sixteenth birthday so they can get their permit to sit behind the wheel. It speaks to them of independence, of being grown up, of taking the first steps up the ladder of adulthood.

Then what does surrendering the driver's license say? Is it the closing down and the end of independence? Does it mean no longer being grown up but having grown old? Does no longer being allowed by law to drive mean they have reached the final rungs on the ladder of adulthood?

After I had asked more than a hundred people about positive aging, I realized that not one of them mentioned anything positive about depending on others.

Is that a weakness in western culture that we don't want to face such a crisis? Is it possible that we've gotten it wrong? Could it be that one of the things we need to accept—*and rejoice in*—is that there are those who care for us and who do it willingly? Is it possible that we can view the dependent stage as a positive aspect to aging?

Before my dad died, he told my mother how much money she needed to have in the bank. "As long as you have that, you won't have to depend on anyone else."

That's a message: We want to hold on to our independence. Dad also wanted Mom to stay by herself and not to have to call on any of us to take care of her. I know others who, like my father, stashed away money so they wouldn't have to lean on anyone else. They often failed to realize (as my dad did) that it's not just about money. After my father died, my mother was unable to live alone. Wanda Yoke, one of my sisters, brought Mom into her home. She loved having her. "Oh we have our differences," Wanda told me. "She thinks I'm too stubborn and I know she's the stubborn one. But we get along fine."

> After I had asked more than a hundred people about positive aging, I realized that not one of them mentioned anything positive about depending on others.

All situations don't work out so neatly. Most of us in the fifty-plus generation pride ourselves on our lack of dependence. But what if God has a different plan for us? What if God wants us to learn to accept help from others? What if God intends us to learn that life is meant as mutual dependence? That's part of the message we read in the Bible and we preach—we care for each other. Most of us like that message—unless we're the ones being cared for.

We like to see ourselves as the Good Samaritan helping

the wounded man by the wayside. We readily acknowledge that God ordains situations where we have the opportunity to be the stranger who helps the wounded. We don't want to think of ourselves as the wounded man by the wayside who depends on the kindness of strangers. Isn't it just as conceivable that God ordains a situation in which other hands help us out of the ditch?

About a year before I started to write this book, I saw this illustrated. Jeff Peterson-Davis, an associate pastor at our church, became quite ill with viral meningitis. He informed the congregation and was on the prayer chain for weeks. After a few months, Jeff said nothing more to the congregation. Severe headaches struck him every day—and some days so bad he couldn't get out of bed. For a number of weeks, Jeff didn't have a well day.

From a source outside our congregation, I learned how sick he was. One Sunday morning, I stopped Jeff in the hallway at church. "You've cheated us out of the opportunity to care about you," I said. "And we love you. You need to let us know so we can care—at least so that we can pray intelli-

> What if God wants us to learn to accept help from others? What if God intends us to learn that life is meant as mutual dependence?

gently for you." I made a point about God's intending that all of us need to be concerned about each other.

After I left him, I thought of what I had said. I meant every word. That is, I meant I wanted to help him and others in need; I didn't want others rushing to help me.

Then it hit me. I was right where many people are. That

was right were *I was*—still living the role of the comforter to the hurting. That's not wrong, but we're not comfortable being comforted.

I didn't understand mutuality. I didn't understand—from the heart—the biblical principle of one body in Christ. Paul writes, "If one part suffers, all the parts suffer with it, and if one part is honored, all the parts are glad" (1 Cor. 12:26 NLT).

I read those words and I nod my assent, but I haven't learned yet how to live in mutuality.

Mutuality means that we extend our hands to give, but we also hold out our hands to receive. What would happen if we learned to depend on others as we have wanted others to depend on us? Wouldn't that be the same as learning to be receivers as well as givers?

> Mutuality means that we extend our hands to give, but we also hold out our hands to receive.

Jesus said, "Freely you have received, freely give" (Matt. 10:8 NIV). In our modern world, many of us have reversed the situation and maybe we need to hear Jesus say it this way, "Freely you have given, now freely receive."

If we accept life as a circle—we start with nothing and end with nothing—it's easier to grasp this. In our early, formative years we receive. When our turn comes to be called adults, we focus on giving. The end of the circle is for us to return to receiving.

By receiving, it doesn't mean to be treated as infants and expect others to do everything for us. We function with the same principle as we did with our children. Most of us refused to do for them what they could do for themselves. We did what they couldn't do. As we age, isn't it time to reverse the procedure? We need help only for what we can't do for ourselves.

I see this beginning to be illustrated in my life. Here are two personal examples. First, I flew to teach at a conference at Mount Hermon, California, in 2003. I lost my wallet (and never found it). I had no money, but I knew I could borrow a few dollars if I needed to buy anything.

At breakfast the next morning, the conference director, Dave Talbott, made a public announcement about my loss and asked for prayer for me. I hadn't asked for prayer and his request embarrassed me.

As soon as we dismissed, a wave of conferees came to me and started to give me "paper handshakes." One man stuffed a ten-dollar bill in my pocket. "No, no, I'm fine," I said and refused the money.

Conferee Ellen List stood in the group and said, "Cec, you're a giver. You have spent your entire life giving to others. Maybe God wants to give back to you; and he's using these people to do it."

She nailed me—lovingly—and she was right. I *allowed* people to give me money—but not very graciously. Only later when I reflected on the experience did I realize how great it felt to be the object of others' compassion.

Second, our son and his wife are both extremely computer literate. I've been using a computer since 1983—but almost exclusively for word processing. I keep learning things from John Mark.

The last time John Mark and Cathie were here, they showed me an easy way to view digital pictures. These days, whenever I encounter a problem with my computer, John or

Cathie can usually tell me how to correct it. This is quite a switch from my taking care of our son.

At this stage of my life, that's as far as my dependency has gone and I don't feel guilty in asking for help. I suspect, however, that if I needed one of my children to drive me to the doctor or take me to buy groceries, I'd feel indebted to them, reluctant to ask, and my dependency on them would incite a negative response from me. I suspect I'd worry about taking up their time and disrupting their lives.

> My wife had exactly the right attitude. It was an opportunity to minister to a loved one in need.

I know better. Shirley and I have done the caregiving part. We kept Edith, an elderly relative, in our home for six and a half years. We took care of her because we loved her and wanted to do what was right for her. Perhaps at our worst moments, we did feel put upon, but those feelings were rare. We believed God wanted us to take care of Edith and allow her to depend on us.

In writing this chapter, I thought of our reaction to Edith. It wasn't always easy, and we had to consider her whenever we made plans for ourselves. I know that if we had the situation presented to us again, we'd still do it gladly.

The caregiving put more of a burden on Shirley than on me, but my wife handled it well. One day she said, "Taking care of Edith is now my primary ministry." My wife had exactly the right attitude. It was an opportunity to minister to a loved one in need.

I understood what Shirley meant and I fully supported her.

But then, we were the caregivers. Reversing the situation by depending on others troubles me. Perhaps that's an issue of pride or American cultural brainwashing. I know it's right—for other people. I struggle with it being right for me. Maybe it's because I don't need the care *yet*. When my time comes to be on the receiving end, however, I want to be able to accept with thanksgiving.

By contrast, I want to tell you about Jimmy Durran. He had been a member of our congregation when I was a pastor on Atlanta's south side. One night on his way home from work, his motorcycle flipped over on an oil slick and he was badly injured. I spent a lot of time with Jimmy during those early months of his recovery. He never fully recovered and remained on disability.

I left the pastorate and didn't see him for another fifteen years. We met in the hallway of a retirement center when I went to visit an elderly friend. Jimmy was seven years younger than I was, but he was living in an assisted living home. A divorcee, he had one daughter and one son. "Why didn't you stay in the Riverdale area so you could be near them?" I asked.

"I didn't want to bother them," he said. "They have their own lives."

"Is that what your kids think or what you think?" I asked. (I'm good at seeing others' problems.)

Jimmy smiled. "Probably me."

Jimmy and I saw each other two or three times before he died of leukemia. I went to the funeral, and both his children were there. His teary-eyed son recognized me, and we talked several minutes. "Daddy wouldn't let me do anything for him," he said. "We begged him to come and live with us, but he was so afraid of being a burden to us."

Afraid of being a burden. Yes, that sounded like Jimmy. That's also how many of us feel. And in some sense, we do become a burden when we depend on others. We disrupt their lives. They would be doing something else if they weren't helping us.

So why should we freely accept and ask for their help?

Maybe it comes down to our lack of graciousness. We feel good when we do things for others. Maybe instead of doing things for others as we age, our role is to receive graciously—and bless them in the process. If we're blessed in the act of giving, perhaps it's time to allow others to be blessed by giving to us.

> We feel good when we do things for others. Maybe instead of doing things for others as we age, our role is to receive graciously—and bless them in the process.

Perhaps we need to learn to prepare ourselves to depend on others. Unless we die suddenly, we will *depend* on others. Perhaps our most gracious, loving, and caring act of giving can be to open our arms in appreciation for what others do for us. And in so doing, we truly bless them. We make their tasks easier because they love taking care of us.

That makes me think of a powerful film called *Driving Miss Daisy.* The story centers on a forty-year period in the life of an aristocratic Jewish woman, played by Jessica Tandy, and her black chauffeur, Hoke, played by Morgan Freeman. In the film's final scene, elderly Miss Daisy is in the nursing home, and her chauffeur visits his former employer. It's

Thanksgiving and she's seated at a table and has finished everything but her dessert. He picks up the fork, cuts a small piece of the pumpkin pie and feeds it to her. She gazes up at him, and her blue eyes sparkle in affection and appreciation. He repeats that twice more. Each time her eyes light up and she smiles at Hoke.

When I saw that film, tears filled my eyes, despite my attempt to push them back. The grateful smile on Jessica Tandy's face communicated far more than a screenwriter's words. Miss Daisy understood the final stage—and smiled in gratitude.

Even though I'm not at that final stage of needing physical care and even though I prefer not to think about the time when it will come, I also want to prepare myself.

We can prepare for dependence. We prepare by learning to be more loving, open, and—wait! That sounds suspiciously like what it means to be a faithful, committed Christian. Maybe that's the final stage in our commitment to God: to joyously and graciously receive from others.

Trusting Myself

Years ago I read a statement by St. Teresa of Avila, in which she stated that the journey to God was also a journey to the self. She referred to it as a movement into self-knowledge.

I've finally begun to understand what she meant. My problem is that for too many years as a Christian, I've quoted and had quoted to me Jeremiah 17:9: "The human heart is most deceitful and desperately wicked. Who really knows how bad it is?" (NLT).

I've lived long enough to admit the perverseness of my own heart. I'm aware that I have a remarkable capacity for self-delusion. Once I accepted the reality that I might be deceiving myself at any time, I decided to learn to trust myself as my next stage of spiritual growth. I've concluded that part of my spiritual growth. That is, I affirm that my relationship with Jesus Christ is secure enough so I can make choices and feel at peace about those choices.

This sounds quite simplistic to write, but it's difficult to achieve.

> I've concluded that part of my spiritual growth is to learn to trust myself.

Because of being aware of my human proclivity to sin and self-deception, I've questioned most of my choices and decisions. In a few instances, I've prayed and God has spoken to me in such a profound way, I've had no doubts.

Those are the exceptions. Most of the times, however, I've prayed, agonized, and questioned the purity of my motives before (and even after) making decisions. This involved anything from buying a new car to the place where God wanted me to worship. I wanted God's will but worried that I might be making a mistake.

I suspect that's about the level where most of us live in our spiritual relationship. We pray and, for lack of clear guidance, we plod along the best we can, and worry (at least a little) if we've done the right thing.

Getting older has helped me think about this differently. I want God's will as much today as ever (and maybe more so). I admit I've made many mistakes—and it's easy to focus on the right choices. I can also say I've made an immense number of correct choices as well.

After all these years. I continue to ask God to direct me, but I rarely agonize as I did for many years. I think of it as reaching a place in my relationship with God where I begin to trust myself.

> I continue to ask God to direct me, but I rarely agonize as I did for many years. I think of it as reaching a place in my relationship with God where I begin to trust myself.

At first, the idea of trusting myself sounded like an ego trip, as if I sought to abandon God. In fact, it's the opposite. It's because I trust my *relationship* with God—because the bond is strong and I've had years to test its strength—I can trust myself. This is what I think St. Teresa meant by self-knowledge. Because I've walked with God since I was twenty-two years old, I'm finally able to have a sense of who God is in my life and to understand myself more clearly.

By contrast, much of what I read in Christian literature is about diminishing ourselves, purging ourselves of pride, self-inflation, and all the other negatives. And I don't want to fool myself that those issues are not real. For too long in my Christian experience, I've focused on those aspects, being fearful and hesitant. My new sense says that I am a child of the heavenly Father and a servant to the Almighty. If God can trust me, why can't I trust myself?

> If God can trust me, why can't I trust myself?

Many of us don't trust ourselves. At an early age we were taught to accommodate those around us, follow rules of behavior, suppress our spontaneous impulses, and do what was expected of us. We also learned to look to outside authorities for answers and directions rather than looking inward and listening to the Holy Spirit.

36

As we age, it means that we respect those other voices, but we've learned to listen to and trust our own voice. That is, our relationship with God is so secure that we pray for guidance and trust ourselves as we listen to the thoughts that come to us as God's answers.

"For most of my life, I depended on others' approval. If they liked what I did, I did more of it," said Karen Rosen. "If they frowned, I turned away. During the past twelve years I've gone through a kind of evolution. My husband died suddenly at age forty-one, and I thought my life was over. I had always depended on him. It took me a few months to pull out of that deep canyon. I don't know if people like me better now (they say they do), but that's no longer my concern. As long as I can approve of myself, I know I'm moving in the right direction. For me—and maybe for everyone— it takes a few years on the body before we can break free of what others think. I'm still a widow, but I'm having more fun than since I was a kid in parochial school. Some mornings I don't make my bed or wash breakfast dishes. I laugh as I dance through my house. I give myself permission to live and to enjoy this life."

>
> As we age, it means that we respect those other voices, but we've learned to listen to and trust our own voice.

After all these years of discipleship, surely God trusts me to do the right thing. If I believe I have the God-given right to make choices, it makes sense that the Giver also encourages me to make wise decisions. If I focus on missing the mark, I become paralyzed or ineffective. Instead, I'm learning to

> I'm learning to say, "My connection with God is strong enough that I'm going to trust myself in making this decision."

say, "My connection with God is strong enough that I'm going to trust myself in making this decision."

My faith in my Creator-Savior is stronger than ever. If I have lost anything, it's the legalistic shackles that kept me earthbound and made me fearful to stand tall as a servant of Jesus Christ. I'm learning to trust my choices instead of cowering in hesitation, anxiety, wondering, worrying, and agonizing.

Learning to trust myself reminds me of my relationship to Shirley. We've been married almost as long as I've been a believer. I know her well. Once in a while she surprises me with a response, but not often. Isn't that the way we assume good marriages work? We know one another's moods, attitudes, beliefs, values, and emotional nuances.

> I'm learning to trust my choices instead of cowering in hesitation, anxiety, wondering, worrying, and agonizing.

If I receive an invitation for both of us for dinner, a social activity, or a play, without asking, I know my wife's response. I discuss the invitation with Shirley and ask what she wants to do, but most of the time, I already know her answer.

Should this be any different in our relationship with God?

It's not that I want to separate myself, which I don't, but it is that I want to act and think with maturity. As I ponder spiritual maturity, it means making right choices God has prepared us to make. After all, isn't that always what maturity means?

Trusting myself isn't only for my benefit. When I trust myself enough to be myself, others respond with their trust. Trust evokes trust. Honesty pulls honesty from others. For me, the more I learn to trust myself the more I can open myself to others and allow

> If I show others a false self and they like what they see, they don't like the true *me*. If they like the unreal me, what happens when they encounter who I truly am?

them to see the real inner me. They may not like who I am and they may not want what I have to offer, but that's the risk I take.

If I show others a false self and they like what they see, they don't like the true *me*. If they like the unreal me, what happens when they encounter who I truly am? Or must I live in constant anxiety that they'll find out who I really am and then they won't like me after all?

Instead, I prefer to think that we recognize others' integrity as ours is recognized. Each of us is more at ease with those we trust. Our vulnerability invites defenselessness. Self-respect encourages respectful behavior toward others, and like a boomerang, it returns to the initiator.

Despite what I've written, I've had a difficult time trusting myself; however, aging gives us perspective. We can look back and remember the times we've followed our own inner guidance. We've not only survived, but we've also grown from the experiences.

If we're not afraid to be our own person—to trust ourselves—eventually we pay attention to our inner feelings.

> Trusting myself isn't only for my benefit. When I trust myself enough to be myself, others respond with their trust.

We come to understand that life's answers lie within us—the deep, inward part where God speaks.

If we don't travel the inner route, we then believe that life's answers lie somewhere outside of us—with some objective authority. We develop the life-long habit of looking to others and asking someone else to show us the way. We think someone else knows better than we do about what's true or best for us. This teaches us to distrust ourselves.

If we live our lives well, we gradually grow into a sense of self-acceptance. We no longer have to compete or to be right, famous, powerful, or even "good." It means not having to impress others. It means we learn to live authentically and with greater integrity.

To trust ourselves means a closer connection with God. Jesus once said to his critics, "I and the Father are one"

> If we don't travel the inner route, we then believe that life's answers lie some-where outside of us—with some objective authority.

(John 10:30 NIV). We can't say that in the same sense he did, of course, but the journey does mean a stronger sense of connectedness—of oneness with God.

One final word about trusting ourselves: I'm convinced that the young can't experience this. The pastor of the first church I ever joined used to say that it was impossible to be a saint without gray hair.

There are lessons we learn only by living, by struggling, by falling, by getting up and trying again, and by staying on the narrow path. The longer we walk the pathway with Jesus Christ, the more we become like our Savior. That is, the more we trust ourselves and rest in our relationship.

> There are lessons we learn only by living, by struggling, by falling, by getting up and trying again, and by staying on the narrow path.

Who Chooses?

Helen, who recently left the workforce, considers taking a nap after lunch. She ponders the matter but she feels extremely conflicted about lying down for an hour. Should she nap or should she water the lawn? Or maybe it would be better use of her time to run an errand. She hasn't finished cleaning the kitchen and bathrooms either.

If she asks Rosa, who lives in the house to the right, her friend would say, "You have earned the right to slow down and take it easy. A nap would be good for you."

If she asks Stella, who lives across the street, she'd hear, "Absolutely not! That's just giving in! It may be only once, but you'll start a pattern and soon you'll have to do it every day. If you give in, you'll shrivel up and sleep your life away. That's what happens to people when they get to the retirement age. They vegetate. Don't let that happen to you."

So what does Helen do? Should she take a nap? Should she push herself to keep on working?

Helen has asked the wrong question. Instead of struggling for a yes or no answer, Helen would benefit more if she asked, "What part of me wants to take a nap?"

Perhaps that sounds like a strange response, but I've found it helpful in many of my decision-making situations when I pause and ask that simple question and listen for the answer. *What part of me wants to say yes?* When I answer myself—and it often demands serious self-searching and reflection—I'll follow a clearer path toward choosing.

When we face inner conflict, as we all do at times, many of us pray, "God, what do you want me to do?" That's not a bad question, but when we have two sides pulling at us, it's difficult to hear God's directions. In fact, I doubt that the Holy Spirit can get a message through, because our inner voices scream at each other.

> *Helen has asked the wrong question.* Instead of struggling for a yes or no answer, Helen would benefit more if she asked, "What part of me wants to take a nap?"

"What part of me wants me to take a nap?" Helen can ask. Then she needs to listen. Is it the stern, self-critical part that fights lying down? an inner voice that rebukes her for being lazy or soft if she gives in? a fear that taking a nap means giving in to old age?

Or could it be the opposite part that's speaking? She's bored and has nothing fun to do. Maybe she's slightly depressed or she's simply tired. By taking a nap, she can get away from all her conflicts for an hour. This part says, "I just want to forget everything and everyone and not worry about problems."

Those are two conflicting sides. The mature part of Helen—if she recognizes the inner conflict for what it is—can make the better choice because she knows the internal arguments. The mature part of Helen could reason, "I've worked rather hard today. I'm feeling slightly tired, and my body needs rest. Once I've rested, I can finish cleaning the house."

> Both sides pull at her. One voice pleads, "Hey, take it easy," and the other demands, "Don't you dare slow down!" For true peace of mind, she needs to learn to cultivate the central position that acknowledges both sides and then she can make a balanced decision.

What Helen needs (and all of us as well) is to take into account that both sides pull at her. One voice pleads, "Hey, take it easy," and the other demands, "Don't you dare slow down!" For true peace of mind, she needs to learn to cultivate the central position that acknowledges both sides and then she can make a balanced decision.

Think again about those two neighbors. They represent the two sides we often find inside ourselves—the stern taskmaster versus the fun-loving and playful. Too often we don't recognize the two clamoring voices and take their desires and needs into account. If we're not careful, they split into warring factions and both strive to control us. Our goal is to cultivate a mature attitude that understands the responsible side without ignoring our fun-loving nature. Otherwise, we get caught between the battle lines. Or as one friend says, "Both sides fight us and then we're really miserable."

If we frequently choose to obey the responsible, task-oriented part, the fun-loving part nags and tries to undermine the other's position. In the end we feel stressed out. If our fun-loving part wins each time, we feel that we're not living up to our potential or doing what we can reasonably expect of ourselves. Thus, we've failed by not doing everything we had planned to do for the day.

When these conflicts stir, we know we're out of balance. This condition says we need to listen—to both sides of our nature—and to cry out for God to help us sort out the conflicts. This conflict—if we're listening to ourselves—forces us to look at our motives and our needs.

I'll give you two personal examples. For many years of my life, I never slept a full eight hours. I continually pushed myself to get by on six. It took me a long time but I finally figured out something. When I was a kid, my father was extremely

> Our goal is to cultivate a mature attitude that understands the responsible side without ignoring our fun-loving nature. Otherwise, we get caught between the battle lines. Or as one friend says, "Both sides fight us and then we're really miserable."

demanding of me. He frequently called me lazy because I didn't work enough for him.

Most of my adult life I realized that I was still listening to Dad's voice call out, "You're lazy." Once I figured out where that voice was coming from, I began to treat myself better. For the past dozen years, I get as much sleep as I need. It's the body's time to repair itself.

Until I learned to listen carefully to my needs (call it my inner voice or my motives or whatever name we choose), I felt conflicted, especially at night or after a long, hard week. One part of me would say, "Rest," and the other would urge, "Don't give in."

> The people-pleaser part of me wanted to affirm the writer; the ethical part of me screamed, "You can't do that!"

The second illustration involves a request from a publisher to write an endorsement for a book by a good friend. They sent the unedited version. By the time I had read through chapter 8, I faced a serious conflict. If I refused to write an endorsement, I'd let my friend down. Maybe hurt his feelings. If I wrote one, I'd feel terrible because, in my opinion, the book wasn't well written.

What should I do? Which voices tugged at me? In this case, it was easy to know the voice, but difficult to make the choice. The people-pleaser part of me wanted to affirm the writer; the ethical part of me screamed, "You can't do that!" Once I knew the realm of conflict, I made my choice—I said no to the publisher.

All of this is a way to say that the peace of Jesus Christ can't flow when we try to say yes to more than one part of ourselves at the same time. It's not that it's wrong to have inner conflicts or different desires. The wrongness (or sin) comes with the refusal to examine ourselves, to listen to both voices, and then choose.

I wonder if that may have been Paul's dilemma when he wrote to the Philippians: "I'm torn between two desires. Sometimes I want to live, and sometimes I long to go and be with Christ" (Phil. 1:23 NLT). He resolved his dilemma—but from the language it sounds as if it's an issue that cropped up regularly. He was able to grasp and acknowledge both types of desires. Then he made his choice: "That would be far better for me [to die], but it is better for you that I live. I am convinced of this, so I will continue with you so that you will grow and experience the joy of your faith" (vv. 23–25).

As we speak of God's peace, we can find it more often if we listen to our inner conflicts and ask the right questions.

Seeing the Future

I used to be intrigued by the promises God gave the people in Old Testament times. I understood part of the promise of fruitful land and prosperity. They were an agrarian culture so it's natural that God would speak to them of such things.

The part that I never understood—until recently—was the part of the promise of long life or living long in the land.

For example, in the Ten Commandments, we read: "Honor your father and mother. Then you will live a long, full life in the land the LORD your God will give you" (Exod. 12:12 NLT).

Paul refers to that same command and adds, "This is the first of the Ten Commandments that ends with a promise. And this is the promise. If you honor your father and mother, you will live a long life, full of blessing" (Eph. 6:2–3 NLT).

These promises appear throughout the Old Testament. Proverbs urges readers to keep God's commands in our hearts "for they will give you a long and satisfying life" (3:2 NLT).

The oft-quoted Psalm 91 ends with the promise to the faithful, "I will satisfy them with long life and give them my salvation" (Ps. 91:16 NLT).

Part of the reason for the long-life part is that the Jews had no concept of eternal life. In fact, the promise of life eternal doesn't appear until the final chapter of the book of Daniel: "Many of those whose bodies lie dead and buried will rise up, some to everlasting life and some to shame and everlasting contempt" (Dan.12:2 NLT).

> The part that I never understood—until recently—was the part of the promise of long life or living long in the land.

Holding out promises of long life—and a blessed, long life—is the highest promise grasped by the saints before Jesus appeared. What made that promise powerful and significant?

I've often said that just to live to an old age means only that we've survived. Among ancient civilizations, however, the hoary head implied wisdom accumulated through years of surviving hardships and difficulties. I understood that.

When I was working on this book, Susan Wales wrote and gave me new insight into the concept of living long. When I asked her for one positive fact about getting older she referred

> Holding out promises of long life—and a blessed, long life—is the highest promise grasped by the saints before Jesus appeared.

to her grandchildren. She says it's not just the joy of becoming grandparents, but more. "There is nothing like seeing my mother's nose, my father's eyes, and my smile on this baby's face, and the joy this baby brings them. Having a baby in the family again is one of the most healing sources of joy one can experience. Introducing the baby to all the beauties and joys of this world allows us to experience life all over again."

Susan e-mailed me months later and wrote, "I just got home last night from visiting my parents. I wept when I read your words because I just spent three weeks experiencing what I wrote with my 86-year-old father and my 76-year-old mother. My granddaughter, their great-grandchild, and her mother were with us and it was amazing. They pointed out features and even personality characteristics about Hailey that reminded them of their parents and grandparents. Now that my parents have more time, I'm sending them some specific scriptures that they can use as they pray for their grandchildren and children every day. This is a great thing for the older generation—praying for their grandchildren, especially blessings on their grandchildren.

"As Carl Sandberg once said, 'Babies are God's opinion that the world should go on.' I couldn't agree more. I wouldn't trade my granddaughter for the wrinkle-free face, the perfect figure, and the no aches and pains era that I enjoyed in my youth. It's worth it all to hear, 'I wuv you Gaga and Bop!' That's heaven."

I read Susan's comments four or five times. They sounded slightly off kilter (and were certainly different from anything else I received in response to my question). Then the words took on sudden (and powerful) meaning when I hooked Susan's comments with the promise of long life in the Old Testament. Now it seems obvious. How could I have missed it? The common way to view life is that most of us will become parents and bring children into the world. Yet we only have to pause to think of the women in the Bible who were barren and how they cried out to God—women such as Sarah, Rachel, and Hannah.

"As Carl Sandberg once said, 'Babies are God's opinion that the world should go on.'"

When Rachel learned she was pregnant she said, "God has removed my shame" (Gen. 30:23 NLT). (Some translations use the word *reproach* instead of *shame*.)

These women did not desire merely to have babies and to repopulate the earth. That was only the beginning. It was not only having children and grandchildren and great-grandchildren, but it was the way people saw their lives as continuing on. It was as if they said, "This is the way I shall live on and perpetuate my life—I shall live through my sons and daughters for generations and generations."

This idea makes even more sense when we think of the Mosaic Law about what happened when a man died childless. His brother was to take the wife as his own and raise children—in the name of the dead brother. This was how they perpetuated the family line, but it was more. It was also a way of living forever.

For example, the book of Genesis ends with the death of Joseph. God commends him for his faithfulness by recording this: ". . . Joseph was 110 years old when he died. He lived to see three generations of descendants of his son Ephraim and the children of Manasseh's son Makir, who were treated as if they were his [Joseph's] own" (Gen. 50:22–23 NLT).

> It wasn't merely to have babies and to repopulate the earth . . . but it was the way people saw their lives as continuing on. It was as if they said, "This is the way I shall live on and perpetuate my life— I shall live through my sons and daughters for generations and generations."

Looking at this from the negative aspect, consider the curses by God. Just before the Israelites went into the Promised Land, Moses reviewed the covenant with them. He enumerated the divine promises, but he also said, "Let none of those who hear the warnings of this curse consider themselves immune . . . the LORD will not pardon such people. His anger and jealousy will burn against them. All the curses written in this book will come down on them, and the LORD will erase their names from under heaven" (Deut. 29:19–20 NLT).

"The LORD will erase their names from under heaven." In our day we quickly skim over that, but to ancient peoples could there have been a more severe curse? They would be cut off and their line would not continue. They would not be remembered. It would be as if they never existed.

That kind of thinking also makes it significant to read

all the genealogical passages scattered throughout the Old Testament and especially the first eleven chapters of 1 Chronicles. It was a way to live in perpetuity through their offspring.

Susan had it right for us in the modern world. Even though we have the assurance of eternal life, like the ancients, long life is for us to see the past in our children—physical features or mannerisms of an earlier generation.

Like Susan, when our children were small, Shirley and I commented on the characteristics each child bore. My parents delighted in pointing out familiar features.

A decade ago, my wife said to me, "The older you get, the more you look like your dad." I have curly hair and all three of my brothers did as well. Our son John Mark has curly hair and so does his son Brett. Those physical characteristics do carry on.

This is just as true with behavioral qualities. When our granddaughter Layla was about a year old, her mother (our second child Cecile) complained about her stubbornness.

I laughed. "It's called payback time," I said. I told Cecile how stubborn she had been as a child. A spanking had no effect (and we spanked in those days). Yes, Cecile's daughter behaved just like her mother. As I smiled gleefully, I remembered that my mother once said to me, "I never broke your will." That's a characteristic that has gone on to at least the third generation.

The idea of long life also implied divine blessings. A common concept was that if people died young, it was because they were wicked and God punished them by snuffing out their lives. Part of the way others saw the reward of the faithful was that they lived many years.

The blessing wasn't merely in longevity but in seeing themselves—their qualities—passed on from generation to generation: their eyes, their height, body size, or curly hair. But it was also the passing on of the blessings of God.

Isn't it possible that it's one form of immortality for us—at least the part of seeing our qualities being passed on to the next generation? If children learn from us and if we present the best, most godly example to them, isn't it natural to expect that they will pass on that attribute as well?

> The idea of long life also implied divine blessings . . . Part of the way others saw the reward of the faithful was that they lived many years.

Susan Wales summed it up beautifully for me: "Maybe that's part of the idea that our immortality on earth comes through those who follow. As we welcome each new generation, we see ourselves in their faces and actions. God promised to bless the righteous to the tenth generation. Maybe part of our blessing is to see parts of ourselves in our children/grandchildren. This also makes us aware of how important it is to us that we reflect the better parts."

How Old Are You?

Of all the people in the Bible, my favorite is Caleb. I've long admired his courage and his faith. My special place of admiration for him is earned after the twelve spies return from Canaan. The Jews had wandered for decades in the wilderness. They didn't have to do that—they could have gone in to conquer the land.

The Bible tells us that Moses sends twelve spies into the Promised Land. They were to bring back a report before the Israelites crossed the Jordan and went into Canaan.

Ten of the spies are frightened of the people and refuse to go forward. "But Caleb tried to encourage the people as they stood before Moses. 'Let's go at once and take the land,' he said. 'We can certainly conquer it'" (Num. 13:30 NLT).

Because of the bad report of the ten and their fearfulness, God makes the people wander for forty years. Because of their faithfulness, Caleb and Joshua are the only adults who left Egypt that are allowed to go into the land.

Recently I thought of Caleb again. He was forty years old when he spied out the land. Forty-five years later, he reminds Joshua, "... I returned and gave from my heart a good report, but my brothers who went with me frightened the people and discouraged them from entering the Promised Land ... " (Josh. 14:7 NLT). Caleb says he "followed the LORD my God completely, so that that day Moses promised me, 'the land of Canaan on which you were just walking will be your special possession and that of your descendants ...' " (v. 9).

> Caleb ... knew his age, and didn't try to hide it or make people think he was younger.... Instead of complaining about how many years he had lived and how many aches and pains he had endured, that man was still alive, healthy, and looking toward the future.

Caleb tells Joshua he is now eighty-five years old. "I am as strong now as I was when Moses sent me on the journey, and I can still travel and fight as well as I could then" (v. 10). So he asks Joshua to give him his inheritance.

What struck me about Caleb is that he had no illusions about his age. He was *eighty-five years old*. I'm not sure he truly was as strong and vibrant as he claimed. We've all heard older folks talk that way. It may be that he hadn't truly acknowledged that his years had sapped his strength and energy.

Regardless, I admire Caleb. He knew his age and didn't try to hide it or make people think he was younger, as we might today. Instead of complaining about how many years he had lived and how many aches and pains he had endured, that man was still alive, healthy, and looking toward the future.

Then another thought occurred to me. What if—instead of thinking of calendar years to measure our lives—we allowed the *quality* of our lives to show our age? What if we allowed our lights to shine to glorify God (see Matt. 5:16) and pointed to the activities of our lives as good indications of our aging?

When I refer to quality, I don't refer to fame or making a lot of money, but rather living a life that counts for God. I think Caleb was like that. He lived his first forty years as a seemingly unimportant man. At least he's not mentioned until he's selected as one of the twelve spies. We know that once the people crossed the Jordan, and although he was then eighty, he continued the fight to drive the enemy out of the Promised Land. We don't know much else about him.

> What if—instead of thinking of calendar years to measure our lives—we allowed the *quality* of our lives to show our age?

Yet we remember him primarily for one thing: He totally followed God. At age eighty-five, he says, in effect, "I'm no different now than I was forty-five years ago when we left Egypt. I'm still following God."

That may be the best way to measure our lives—by the spiritual distance we've covered and not by the years we've tallied up. It's just possible that true spirituality doesn't

> That may be the best way to measure our lives—by the spiritual distance we've covered and not by the years we've tallied up.

really happen until the gray hairs start multiplying, until we've lived long enough to allow the light of a lifetime to shine and bring glory to God. Conversions to Christ are exciting, and we often celebrate them in our churches. What would it be like if we celebrated the life and commitment of those who fully followed the Savior for fifty years? or seventy? Those are the real testimonies of a faith that endures.

Maybe part of getting older is to be able to speak not only of surviving all the hardships in life, but also of triumphing in the midst of them. What would it be like if we measured our lives, not by years, but by the important things we've accomplished. When former President Bush was asked about his greatest accomplishment, he said, "My family." That's the way to count our aging process—by our families, our service for God, and our walk with Jesus Christ.

Even there we sometimes trip up and see service only as preaching or missionary service, but that's not what I mean. I think of Leona and Ross Jenkins, who moved to the Atlanta area and joined our church in Riverdale when both were in their seventies. About the fourth Sunday after they joined, Leona came to me and said, "Ross and I want to be official greeters." Just that—and they began their ministry.

Until they moved four years later, every Sunday, Ross and Leona stood at the church door and warmly greeted every person who came inside. That's service. Maybe that's the kind of measurement we need to use when we think about how old we are.

At the Riverdale church the membership doubled during our first five years in our pastorate there, and most of the new ones were people under thirty. We had growth, but I also realized that we did so many things for our younger members, I was afraid we were going to neglect our older members. I started meeting with the older members every month. At least once a year, we planned a special time in our worship service when we honored those who had been part of the church for a long time. We started out by calling out the names of those who had been members more than fifty years.

The church was founded in 1895 and I wanted the younger and newer members to realize that those who had been there since those early days had set the pace. "They have made possible the good things about the church and the fellowship we enjoy today."

Another time when our elders discussed whether to build an all-purpose building for more Sunday school classrooms, one of the oldest members of the church, Alton Adams, asked to say something.

I stared at him and assumed he was going to oppose the building. He told us that he had been in the church since he was a baby. He recounted many things the church had gone through, including once when the wooden frame building burned to the ground. Finally he said, "If there's one mistake we made again and again it was that we never made the rooms large enough. Let's build, but this time, let's make sure we make it large enough."

Alton was in his eighties then, but he still had insight and was able to think futuristically.

> Instead of emphasizing careers or personal achievements, what would it be like if we began our timeline with our conversion to Jesus Christ and marked the years by our service and commitment?

Another way for us to ponder our age is to write out a timeline. Instead of emphasizing careers or personal achievements, what would it be like if we began our timeline with our conversion to Jesus Christ and marked the years by our service and commitment?

I did this once and called it my life's "age markers." The first marker was my baptism at age twenty-two. A year later, I began to teach an adult Sunday school class. That same year, my wife and I saw a need in the youth department and for two years, we became the official youth advisors. None of those were big things or the types of service that anyone else would think much about. Not big in themselves, but they show my age markers. They speak of my journey and mark my spiritual steps. I also saw that as we were faithful in our service, God entrusted us with greater opportunities.

> Caleb . . . may have looked back long enough to see where he had been, but the rest of the time he looked forward to where he was going.

That's how I see Caleb functioning. He may have

looked back long enough to see where he had been, but the rest of the time he looked forward to where he was going.

When I come to the end of my spiritual journey, I'd like to have it said of me as it was of Caleb that I had ". . . wholeheartedly followed the Lord my God." My age won't matter very much. What I did with my life is what will count. And if I live uprightly, that's what will count.

Sharing What
We Know

M*zee* was one of the first words I learned when
we lived in Africa. The Swahili word means
"old man," but it implies much more. At the
time we lived in Kenya, Jomo Kenyetta was the president
and everyone referred to him as *mzee*. For the Africans,
the title was more than having wrinkles and white
hair—it also implied deep respect. They honored such
individuals and listened to their accumulated wisdom.

Many ancient people considered elders as the hold-
ers of wisdom in the culture. They had more knowledge
and a long history of experience—it's not mere knowledge, but a matter of *applied knowledge.* Not all older
people are wise, of course, but it's what some might call
an intuitive knowledge. Wisdom means knowing how

to respond properly to a given situation. Much of that ability comes from having lived a number of years.

> Many ancient people considered elders as the holders of wisdom in the culture.

When young, we strive for "tribal goals"—what the culture calls normal—such as continuing our education, landing a good job, getting married, and raising a family. As we get older we carry our experienced learning and we can pass it on to others.

"Finally people take me seriously," said Eva Marie Everson: "When I hit thirty, I was looked at as too old by those younger than me and not quite old enough by those who were older. But past age forty-five I've suddenly become wise. People come to me for advice."

By contrast, I like the saying of ancient Roman philosopher Seneca: "Nothing is more dishonorable than an old man, heavy with years, who has no further evidence of having lived long, except his age."

I vividly recall the first time I connected wisdom with my own life. My writer-friend, Marlene Bagnull, e-mailed asking my advice, and I responded with a rather simple and (to me) obvious answer. I even wrote a brief apology for not having any great insight to offer.

> I like the saying of ancient Roman philosopher Seneca: "Nothing is more dishonorable than an old man, heavy with years, who has no further evidence of having lived long, except his age."

> I find it difficult to write this (for fear of sounding boastful), but years of living and learning surely must have amounted to some kind of accumulated value.

While I waited for her reply, I berated myself for the inability to give her the profound responses I yearned for her to have. I didn't know how to solve her immediate problem and wished I had more to offer. I wondered if my comments had made the situation worse. Not that I had given bad advice, but she wanted help. What if my answer had further frustrated her?

Later that day, she responded by e-mail, telling me my words were exactly what she had needed to hear, and added that those few sentences had opened a door of insight. "It was something I hadn't considered before," she wrote.

My words had helped her? How was that possible? They had seemed so simple and obvious. Tears filled my eyes, and I replied, "If you had been here when I read your e-mail, you would have seen an old man cry."

While I was still online with other e-mails, she responded with these words: "Old man? You're not old! Besides, you are incredibly wise, and you have so much common sense. What a blessing you've been to me!"

Shock waves raced through my brain. A blessing? I had been a blessing? I felt immensely grateful for those kind words.

For the next few days I pondered what Marlene had written. Aside from the obvious compliment, I needed to reflect on the implications of her words. That woman, maybe fifteen years younger than I am, didn't focus on our age difference, and she considered only the words I had to offer.

I find it difficult to write this (for fear of sounding boastful), but years of living and learning surely must have amounted to some kind of accumulated value. I hadn't been exactly where Marlene was, but I had been in situations with enough similarity to make several observations. To me, they were obvious; to her, profound.

To put it another way, my advice blessed her—encouraged and strengthened her to push forward. Then I thought of several other incidents where I had responded to friends in their need. I was touched when they asked for my opinion or as one person put it, "your counsel."

Is it possible, I asked God, that by reflecting on my experiences through years of living, I can share my insights and be a blessing? Could it be because I'm older and have known a few more of life's battles, that Marlene and others have chosen to ask me for advice?

Perhaps I felt shocked because of my feelings of inadequacy, or maybe the possibility of having practical and wise things to say staggered me. Over the next few days, I gradually accepted one fact: God could use my efforts to bless others. I had accumulated some wisdom through more than a half-century of being alive, even though I didn't think my comments were particularly insightful.

> Is it possible, I asked God, that by reflecting on my experiences through years of living, I can share my insights and be a blessing?

Since that incident in 2000, I've recognized that wisdom truly is a special gift of aging. It means that we've taken the risks. We've made bad decisions, learned from them, and

> Wisdom truly is a special gift of aging. It means that we've taken the risks. We've made bad decisions, learned from them, and now we can make better decisions.

now we can make better decisions. Aged wisdom means that we can see more objectively because we're not living in the middle of every situation or every problem.

"It has often been said that there is only one way to gain experience. With that in mind, a positive aspect of aging is having many years of experience to apply to living," wrote Robert Carpenter. "An example of this is that when our son, Mark, was thirty, a situation arose where he did not agree with Janet and me. I asked him, 'When you were fifteen, half your current age, would you have felt differently?' He said, 'Of course.' I responded, 'When I was thirty, which is half of my current age of sixty, I felt much as you do. But, since I have had thirty years of experience that you have not had, I feel differently.' He understood and took our advice."

Reaching fifty or sixty or any other age doesn't automatically induct us into the Hall of Wisdom. Getting older does, however, give us the *opportunity* to share our experiences, as well as to reflect on the lessons we've learned from accumulated pain, failures, and triumphs.

Reaching that status of "older" carries with it opportunities for enriching others. It's like having reached the summit of Mount Everest—a perspective gained after many painful slips, falls, scrapes, and narrow escapes. We can sit and bask in the sunlight, fret over the things we hated about the trip up, or we can use our energies to assist other climbers on their way to the summit.

We didn't have a map to guide us to the top, and there's no way we can honestly say, "If you'll just follow what I did, you'll make it without bumps and scrapes." Somehow we've accomplished our journey—or at least we're getting close to the summit—and we may feel amazed that we're as far along as we are. I suspect if we're honest, we'll also say that at several difficult bends along the circuitous journey we benefited from the older-but-still-strong voices ahead. "Come on. Try this path," they said. "You can make it. Don't give up." Maybe they gave us the emotional boost or spoke the words of encouragement we needed right then.

> Reaching fifty or sixty or any other age doesn't automatically induct us into the Hall of Wisdom. Getting older does, however, give us the *opportunity* to share our experiences, as well as to reflect on the lessons we've learned from accumulated pain, failures, and triumphs.

For a week after Marlene's second e-mail, I thought about that matter of being a blessing. What a wonderful opportunity God has given me. I'm alive. I've survived thus far, and now in my declining years (I hate to say "declining," but I am on the downward path), I can bless others.

What a powerful thought, and she pushed me to accept myself more fully. No matter how insignificant I may be in the world, I can be a "blesser" for God. I have the unique opportunity to guide those who are still below and are traveling on the stony, irregular path.

We don't have to be wise or feel wise. I'm still not sure I said anything profound to Marlene, but I've learned that we bless most when we give what we have. It doesn't mean that we offer advice that they must follow. Rather, we share our insights and leave them free to accept or toss aside our words.

Maybe that's wisdom in itself—to make suggestions to those younger and allow them the freedom *not* to follow our words.

Mississippi pastor William Patterson said that wisdom "means the kind of experience that enables me to know that if something does not work out, it is not the end of the world. As a young minister, if something I proposed to the church did not fly, I would be devastated. Now I am not. Experience is the key difference. I know if one thing does not work, there is a reason and God will help me go about the needed change another way. Having had this kind of experience helps me to lay out a plan and why I think it is best, but at the same time to affirm others that they are also children of God and have good minds and hearts and maybe they can come up with a better way.

> No matter how insignificant I may be in the world, I can be a "blesser" for God. I have the unique opportunity to guide those who are still below and are traveling on the stony, irregular path.

"This allows people to respond to the pull and direction of the Holy Spirit on their lives and not to my powers of persuasion. The end result is that people sometimes come up with better alternatives than I could have imagined. And if they choose to go with what I propose, it is because they genuinely think it is the best option."

As we age, we accumulate knowledge and learn to apply what we've learned. That's wisdom. We may doubt our wisdom and think of ourselves as only speaking words of common sense. But isn't common sense another term for the wisdom lacked by those without experience?

> Maybe that's wisdom in itself—to make suggestions to those younger and allow them the freedom *not* to follow our words.

My friend, Don Renner, summed this up nicely: "For me, aging means the opportunity to understand all of the good and bad things that happened to me when I was younger. Forcing that understanding on others with the expectation that it's what they ought to know or what they should do defeats their freedom to grow."

Someone else said, "Experience isn't to tell others what they ought to know or what they should do. It is to pass on life without judgment and with compassion, and to enjoy life now."

One of the wisest responses I received came to me from Patti Patterson of Sarasota, Florida, and she called it "Five Pounds of Ashes."

"I never thought I was getting older until my husband's 85-year-old mother died from a massive stroke. She had left instructions for cremation and

> "Aging means the opportunity to understand all of the good and bad things that happened to me when I was younger."

that was done. She also left instructions about spreading her ashes at the ocean.

"I had never seen human ashes before and was astounded when my husband carried a five-pound cardboard box to the beach at twilight. We added our own touches of Scripture and prayers, thanking God for her life and influence. Then my husband scattered his mother's ashes across the lapping waves.

> WISDOM
> "~~Experience~~ isn't to tell others what they ought to know or what they should do. It is to pass on life & *my wisdom* without judgment and with compassion, and to enjoy life now."

"I was struck with how short life is and how it boils down to five pounds of light gray ashes. I came away with a deep resolve to make sure my life counted. Whether God gave me one day or many days, it has become vital that I do what is important to Him.

"How does this relate to positive aging? I think my life has taken on a new and truer meaning. What kind of legacy am I leaving? What kind of impact am I having for my Savior? Then, aging does not become so much numbers but impact. Ashes or impact. I choose impact."

Reconnecting

Something happens to most people when they hit those middle-to-late years. An inborn desire rushes into their lives to reconnect with their past.

For example, every five years our high school graduating class holds a reunion. The attendance dragged along until the fiftieth anniversary (and my friends say this is typical). That reunion brought the biggest turnout ever.

Why that one? Why not the twenty-fifth or the fortieth? I'm not sure, but I suspect it has to do with looking backward ("I've survived") and feeling isolated ("I need connections to people I've known for a long time") and maybe even a sense that holding the hand of a contemporary makes the last steps a little easier. It's also what I call reconnecting.

> An inborn desire rushes into their lives to reconnect with their past.

As a former pastor, I used to see this reconnecting occur among siblings after the death of both parents. Was it awareness that they themselves had now become the older generation? Was it a sense of having lost their connectedness to their origins that made them yearn to clasp the hands of their brothers and sisters? Could it be that those reconnections stemmed from a sense of facing the end of their lives and wanting to bring childhood into the picture again?

I don't know, and perhaps it's a combination of all those reasons. I'm aware, however, that growing older has some kind of built-in genetic yearning to go back and restore the broken walls of relationships. This may mean contacting friends from childhood, people we dated in high school or college, or those we worked with in our twenties.

My friend, *Eddie, went to his fiftieth high school reunion and was surprised at the huge turnout. His class of more than five hundred graduates has reunions every five years and he's been to all of them.

> Growing older has some kind of built-in genetic yearning to go back and restore the broken walls of relationships.

One of the people he sought out was Donna, whom he had dated as a senior and even a few months after graduation. Both had married other people. They hadn't seen each other during all those years, even though they lived in the same large city.

"I didn't feel anything for Donna," he said. "It wasn't that I expected to feel any romance rekindling. Maybe it was just a desire to see her. Maybe it was to assure myself that I hadn't made a mistake in breaking up with her."

As I listened to Eddie, I wondered if this is part of some kind of circle effect—we move out of our teen years in a variety of ways and make our way in the world and the circle gets wider. Going back puts closure to the circle. Is it like leaving home, going out into the world to make our fortunes, and then at some point feeling the need to return home again? We're not the same and neither is anyone we left behind, but we're still drawn back by some inner force that we may not even understand.

My awareness of this became clear when Dad was nearly eighty and his health was failing. He and my mother drove from Iowa to Oklahoma where they had lived the first half of their lives. From there they drove on to Southern California to see several still-surviving friends. Just before he left, Dad said, "This is the last trip I'll ever take."

Because of his health, he probably shouldn't have driven that far, but it was almost as if he made the journey without a choice—as if some inner compulsion had taken hold of him. I wondered at the time if that might not just be part of human destiny. He died two years later.

> I wondered if this is part of some kind of circle effect—we move out of our teen years in a variety of ways and make our way in the world and the circle gets wider. Going back puts closure to the circle.

Chuck White, who is fifty, told me about the pleasure of enjoying old friendships. "And the only way to have them comes through years of relationship." He met his best friend in fourth grade. The best friendships need time to mature. Not only in their affection but in understanding and commitment.

Here's another example: Eighty-year-old Frank Brackett drove to visit his younger sister, who lived fifteen hundred miles away. He brought two large photo albums with him. Their first night together, his conversation began with, "Do you remember . . . ?" For the next five evenings, that was his favorite question.

Frank couldn't always remember to take his daily medication, and driving directions sometimes confused him, but he clearly remembered stories of the family when he was a boy.

> As we age, our short-term memory decreases, but we seem to compensate by long-term memories of childhood—as if God has stored them in a secret vault that we can finally reopen and enjoy.

As we age, our short-term memory decreases, but we seem to compensate by long-term memories of childhood—as if God has stored them in a secret vault that we can finally reopen and enjoy. One of my older friends says they come back with such a clarity it's as if they had happened only weeks earlier.

I have no idea why it works that way. Here's my theory: It's the conclusion of the circle. In a way, we're all like the hero of the tales, who left home for the larger world. When we've done all our brave deeds (or just survived the years), it's time to go home again.

No matter what they say, we *can* go home again. It's not the home we left; but it has become the place of treasured memories. It's the place where we revisit the past and smile. We remember carving our initials in the oak tree in the backyard. We recall that our street then had only two traffic signals between our house and our school. We stare at buildings as they are, but we can still envision how things once were.

"See those stores over there? When I was a boy, those were our cotton fields," eighty-year-old Alton Adams once said. "We didn't have any money back then, but we had the land."

"Do you miss the cotton fields?" I asked. (I was forty years old at the time.)

Alton stared into the sky, and at first I thought he wasn't going to answer. Then he said in a soft voice, "Just about every day. Just about every day."

I wonder if, even then, Alton wasn't reconnecting to his childhood days.

Reconnecting also makes me wonder about God's ultimate purpose in this activity. Is it part of our preparation for the future?

Reconnecting also makes me wonder about God's ultimate purpose in this activity. Is it part of our preparation for the future? I wonder if going back and reconnecting isn't God's way to whisper, "You've had a full life. You've gone from the cradle through all the troubles and joys that life has to offer. Now it's time to move on to the final stage."

Then perhaps God silently impresses us that by our reconnecting, we'll be able to see our life in its entirety. We see what we were, where we've been, and as Christians, we know where we're going.

> By our reconnecting, we'll be able to see our life in its entirety. We see what we were, where we've been, and as Christians, we know where we're going.

Is it possible that only by reconnecting and going back to the earliest times we can complete the circle?

In the mythological tales, the hero goes out into the world, slays dragons and defeats evil, and after he's won all the battles and slain all the evil monsters, he returns home again. He's the same person and yet he's also different. He has lost his innocence, but he hasn't lost his love for the friends of childhood. He's wiser, more experienced, and understands mysteries. He leaves as the innocent and returns as the wise.

> "Life must be understood backward. But it must be lived forward."

Isn't that also a picture of real life? The older people become, the more powerful this need seems to stir them. Perhaps this is the divinely given opportunity for us to say as my friend Jeff Turner remarked, "Yes, I have lived a full life. Taken as a whole, it has been a good life."

Taken as a whole. That's the way life truly makes sense. Or as Søren Kierkegaard put it, "Life must be understood backward. But it must be lived forward." [3]

That makes sense out of our need to reconnect.

Making Faces

Years ago I read a statement that went something like this: The face you have at age twenty is the one you were born with. Your face at age forty is who you are becoming. Your face at age sixty is the face you deserve.

There must be something to that. It's not just our physical appearance, but also our personalities and our outlook. I began to grasp that rather clearly after Shirley visited Edith when she was in a skilled nursing facility. Edith was sweet and quiet, but the nurses had a variety of problems with Estelle, Edith's roommate. The woman yelled at everyone and showed no patience with any of the staff. Most days she pulled her wheel-chair to the door and blocked the entrance. She refused to let anyone inside, and they had to forcefully push her away to get inside—or to get back out.

One day, the head nurse came into the room and told Shirley how much everyone loved Edith. "She is one of the sweetest people I've ever known. A few times her meals have been late or we've been a little slow in bringing in her medication, but she has never complained. Even when she's in pain, she always has a smile for everyone."

> The face you have at age twenty is the one you were born with. Your face at age forty is who you are becoming. Your face at age sixty is the face you deserve.

Estelle's daughter was in the room and heard the conversation. Shirley then said, "I suppose your mother has so much pain that it must be difficult for her to smile about everything."

The woman shook her head. "My mother hasn't changed. She was always difficult to get along with. The older she gets, the worse she becomes."

When Shirley related that story to me, the daughter's remarks made sense. When we reach seventy-five, we don't suddenly change into a cantankerous individual. Isn't it true that we live out the personality that we've been forging all through our lives?

The more I've considered those words, the more I realize the importance of a daily, ongoing walk with Jesus Christ and a constant self-evaluation. I believe in eternal life, and I believe that after death we reap the rewards for our labors. Those are good reasons for following the way of Jesus Christ. Another good reason for obeying our Lord is that our actions make us into the people we're becoming. That is, we can choose now the people we want to be when we reach the end of our lives. We don't have to allow anger, frustration, or jealousy to control and condition us.

> Another good reason for obeying our Lord is that our actions make us into the people we're becoming.

We actually make those life-shaping decisions fairly early. For instance, if we scrutinize people when they're twenty, we can already see the patterns of their lives emerging. By the time they reach their middle years, those patterns, habits, and values have become fairly well ingrained. Of course, people can change, and God works miracles. For the most part, however, we continue to reinforce that which we have already begun.

We're people in progress, individuals under construction, and we're following the blueprint we selected. We can blame heredity, our parents, lack of opportunities, but reality indicates that although we can't change our circumstances, we can choose our outlook.

> People can change, and God works miracles. For the most part, however, we continue to reinforce that which we have already begun.

Another way to say it is that those who are kind and loving tend to become kinder and more loving as they get older. But that doesn't happen automatically. Somewhere they have had to choose to reflect such traits. Generally speaking, whoever we are at any stage in our lives depends on our reactions to the events in life. Those events, in turn, continue to propel us forward and help complete our own self-portrait.

As an illustration, for several years, I regularly ate lunch with a friend, *Vincent, who was sixty-two years old. We used to have delightful fellowship, but over the years, his tone darkened and his negative conversation became predictable. My simple, "How are you?" meant hearing a lengthy physical report. Vincent moaned about his high cholesterol or discussed the side effects of his high blood-pressure medication, and he complained that his heart medicine wasn't strong enough.

> Those who are kind and loving tend to become kinder and more loving as they get older. But that doesn't happen automatically.

He detested his job; he told me about it in painful detail—and I didn't have to ask. By the time our main course had arrived, his horrible work situation had become the major topic. He'd go through the litany of everything wrong in his job environment.

I liked Vincent, and once we got past his problems, we had excellent conversations, because he was witty and well read.

About a year ago, however, I silently ate my salad and let him go through his lengthy complaint. When he paused, I asked, "Why do you stay there? You could take an early retirement."

"I'd lose my stock options," Vincent said, and then went on to explain, as if I were fifteen years old, the good retirement benefits he would have in three more years.

I had heard all of that before too, and I blurted out, "The way your life is going you won't be able to enjoy your retirement anyway." As soon as I spoke, I realized I shouldn't have said those words, although I'd thought them a dozen times. They were unkind. Too late, I tried to smooth it over with, "Why don't you spend your last three working years doing something you enjoy?"

The avalanche of his anger fell on me, and his blast of words called me everything from insensitive to judgmental and mean-spirited. At one point, he called me jealous for not making as much money as he did.

Later, I called to apologize for hurting his feelings, and he mumbled an acceptance. For the next couple of months, he always had something else to do when I called. That lunch a year ago was the last time I ever saw Vincent.

By contrast, I thought of Psalm 37, purportedly written by David. He wrote, "Once I was young, and now I am old. Yet I have never seen the godly forsaken, nor seen their children begging for bread" (Ps. 37:25 NLT). That's the positive attitude of a man who'd seen a lot of hardship, deprivation, and his life had been in danger many times. David had also known God's presence and pleasure since childhood. He was a teen when he killed Goliath.

The man spent many of his adult years fleeing the murderous wrath of King Saul. Through all those years of hardship, he remained a man with a passion for God. As he aged, David continued to paint his portrait of an individual who hungered after God.

Here we are, thousands of years later, painting our portraits. The good thing is that, even though we have sketched in our picture, we can paint outside the lines or redo some of the parts. We may not be able to change everything, but we can lift the drooping corners of our lips or widen our smile. We can learn to focus on pleasant thoughts and not fill our minds with gossip or negative thoughts. We can forgive others and thrust away our grudges.

Eleanor Roosevelt said that beautiful young people are accidents of nature, but beautiful old people are works of art.

That we can make those changes and become works of art is a benefit of growing older. That's when we slow down. That is, because we're forced to cut down on our speed and we don't have energy to take on as many activities or stay at them as long, we're able to become more reflective—if we make that choice. Something about the aging process that God has put into our hard drive pushes us to look backward and reflect on our past. That reflective time can be an opportunity to reevaluate and to alter the otherwise inevitable future.

I started this chapter by telling about our faces at ages twenty, forty, and sixty. However, I'd like to add that our faces at eighty are what we have *chosen* to *make* them.

I'll tell you exactly the kind of face I'd like to have when I reach my eighties. I'd like people to notice my smile wrinkles. I'd like them to sense from the brightness of my eyes

> Eleanor Roosevelt said that beautiful young people are accidents of nature, but beautiful old people are works of art.

that I've lived a joyful and contented life, and that somehow they'll sense that Jesus has walked by my side every day through the years.

The final thing I want people to say about me is this: "Cec died with a smile on his face."

That, for me, will be the perfect face.

No Longer Listening

Although several friends hold a variety of college degrees, they suffer from miseducation. They've read the major studies on aging and know exactly what they can expect at each milestone in their lives. Mostly they seem to know what they can't do and the restrictions they need to place on themselves.

Here are two examples. I'm a runner and have been running since the 1970s. Recently someone asked, "Are you *still* running?"

When I told her I was, she pointed out that I shouldn't be doing that "at your age." She gave me a ninety-second lecture on learning to accept my age and not trying to "act like you're still young." After all, she had read several books about taking care of ourselves after age fifty.

I didn't argue with her. She knew so much about what people shouldn't do that she seemed unable to appreciate that I was still running and loving it.

The second example involves *Max who contacted me. "I want to write—it's something I've always wanted to do and now I have the time to learn and focus." I worked with him for several weeks, but he didn't show much progress.

> Although several friends hold a variety of college degrees, they suffer from miseducation.

"You just can't teach old dogs new tricks," he said. "After all, I'm sixty-three."

"Don't play the age card with me," I said and detected testiness in my voice. "I'm older than you are and I'm still learning." I went on to say that if he wanted to blame his lack of progress on not being motivated to learn, that was all right, but I refused to accept getting old as the reason he couldn't learn to write.

Then he complained that no one wanted to read anything by an old man like him.

"You have a lot more to share with the world now than you did when you were twenty," I said. "What did you know about life when you were thirty? How much have you learned since then?"

> I refused to accept getting old as the reason he couldn't learn to write.

Max didn't persevere as a writer—he had listened to too many negative voices. "They said" he was too old, too set in his ways to learn new things, or too out of date to offer anything practical to readers today.

Too many listen to those voices that tell them to slow down and ease up. Why is it, I wonder, that those who make the most noise about slowing down are those who haven't done anything new or shown

> I'm not living my life by someone's predictability charts or educated explanations. I'm wearied with people who use ageism as an excuse.

any signs of growth themselves? Is it possible that they want me to listen to them, so I'll vegetate as well?

As for me, I'm no longer listening to those voices. I'm not living my life by someone's predictability charts or educated explanations. I'm wearied with people who use ageism as an excuse.

I hear excuses and explanations and I want to shout, "Listen to your body. Let your own mind tell you when to slow down or give up activities. As long as you have the desire and the physical endurance, stay with it."

Isn't it time for radical reeducation in the area of aging? We tend to think of exploration and discovery as the domain of the young, but isn't it possible that it is just as much for older adults? We swallow all the stereotypes such as brittle bones, constipation, depression, and narrow thinking. Instead, isn't it possible that we can focus on aging as a time to strengthen our individual faith and be living examples of Christianity?

Immediately, I think of Bud Ferguson who entered seminary at age fifty-five with plans to become a pastor.

Someone said to him, "By the time you finish, you'll only have seven years before you'll have to retire."

"True, but I'll have seven years that I can serve as a pastor. That's seven years!"

> We tend to think of exploration and discovery as the domain of the young, but isn't it possible that it is just as much for older adults?

My agent Deidre Knight used to live in Atlanta, about fifteen minutes' drive from us. She and her family moved into a small town approximately an hour away. Her husband Jud e-mailed me about his coming into the city and having lunch with me. I wrote back something about visiting "the 'hood again."

Thirty-something Jud responded by saying that he didn't know anyone else my age who knew how to use that term for neighborhood.

This isn't to suggest we need to clutch at every new term that comes along. (I didn't do that when I was thirty either.) It does mean staying abreast of language and what's going on in the world around us. I may not recognize the music of Eminem or be able to sing along with LeAnn Rimes, but at least I know who they are.

I also know that if I want the world to treat me as decrepit and senile, all I need to do is show them that kind of face. If we're open, excited about life, and ready to grasp new things, we don't have to tell people: They'll figure out who we are as they interact with us. Even without being told, when we interact with others, we sense who's alive and still climbing mountains. We also know those who've given up and lie down alongside the path.

Isn't it time for us to stop listening to those other voices that seem to know what's best for us?

I caught on to this principle when I was a pastor in my forties. I made it a practice to visit shut-ins regularly. Our congregation observed the Lord's Supper the second Sunday of every month. During the week following, I contacted all our shut-ins and offered to bring the sacrament to them. Unless they were too ill, they welcomed me.

The attitudinal differences amazed me, and it had nothing to do with age. For instance, Mae Cook, who was almost ninety, wore a bright red wig. "I love that color and since I don't have enough of my own hair, why not get a color I like? No matter what color, everyone knows it's a wig. So I'm going to enjoy my red hair."

This isn't to suggest we need to clutch at every new term that comes along. (I didn't do that when I was thirty either.) It does mean staying abreast of language and what's going on in the world around us.

I was her pastor for almost a decade. Only one time did she turn me down and that was because she and her *older* sister had something planned. "The Braves are playing this afternoon and we want to watch the game. Could you come tomorrow?"

I loved that response. By their sprightly interest in baseball, those two women remained alive, enjoyed keeping their world open, and they didn't listen to anyone who told them they were too old to enjoy professional baseball.

Here's another illustration from that same time period. The leader of the high school group asked the kids to select the most spiritual and influential person in the church (they couldn't pick the pastors). Almost unanimously, they picked a woman named Anne Dunivin. She didn't work in the youth department. All her activities involved the adults of the church. She taught the Sunday school class for the older members. Oh, and at the time, Anne was in her mid-sixties.

When she heard that the students had named her, she was amazed. I wasn't; the teens knew.

That's the point I want to make: Anne continued to grow, remain active, and she set the example.

By contrast, I can think of a woman who was about the same age in the same church. Several times I asked her for help, such as the time I asked her to substitute one Sunday for the kindergarten class. "I taught Sunday school for over thirty years," the woman said. "Now it's someone else's turn."

That woman hasn't been to church in years (I've been told) and her health has been in serious decline, whereas Anne remains an active member.

Obviously, there are many factors involved, but I thought of the difference between Anne and the other woman when I read about a study released by the University of Chicago in December of 2003 in which they wrote about stress, health, and longevity. Although they couldn't explain the reason, they know that animals with an innate phobia of novelty have higher levels of stress hormones after new experiences. They also die significantly younger. The studies go on to say that these results apply to people as well. Individuals who are afraid of trying new things tend to die younger.

> "People who need people are not just lucky; they may be healthier too."

Time magazine's article, "Why Men Should Make More Friends," said that "people who need people are not just lucky; they may be healthier too."[4] The brief article went on to point out that socially isolated men in their seventies appear to be more susceptible to heart disease than those with a more robust social network.

It's more than having a social network—it's remaining a vital part of life as it goes on around us and being part of what goes on.

What would life be like if all of us over fifty saw life as a time of exploration? a time to learn new things and to grow? As I wrote those words, I know many who see it as just the opposite. The experts point out that it's a time for closing down and for putting away our options.

Then I thought of a lovely couple named Leonard and Marilyn Auton, who are excellent ballroom dancers. I loved to watch them dance and their faces showed me how much they enjoyed the music.

The last time I chatted with them, Leonard had just celebrated his seventy-fifth birthday. "When did you start dancing?" I asked.

"When I retired," he said.

That couple didn't listen to the negative voices.

Healthy aging means the courage to release stereotypical ideas. We can open ourselves to curiosity, and we can take the time to more fully explore our inner and outer world. We can make aging an invitation into another way of life.

I ran into this quotation recently by Jeannette Clift-George: "Youth is grossly overrated and maturity is grossly underrated. I have aged past a lot of things that were limiting."

Isn't it time for us to stop listening to all those voices who want to hinder us from living life to the fullest? I can only speak for myself, but I'm no longer listening to those negative voices.

> "I am still not all I should be, but I am focusing all my energies on this one thing: Forgetting the past and looking forward to what lies ahead."
> —Phil. 3:12–13, NLT

I'm committed to the attitude of the imprisoned Paul when he wrote to the Philippians. At the time, he didn't know if he would live or die, but he wrote, "I keep working toward the day when I will finally be all that Christ Jesus saved me for and wants me to be. No, dear friends, I am still not all I should be, but I am focusing all my energies on this one thing: Forgetting the past and looking forward to what lies ahead" (Phil. 3:12–13, NLT).

That's a voice I want to listen to.

Growing older is part of life.
Journey that where we are further
sanctified and changed to be
who christ wants us to be.

Valuing Life

*M*alignancy. That word stuck in my throat.

As a pastor, I had used it many times and helped others work through their struggles with what that term meant. Now my turn had come to say the word aloud about my wife.

Shirley examined her breasts monthly. One day she felt a hard lump. That same morning, she called her doctor. After a series of tests, he used that terrible word, and we learned she needed a radical mastectomy.

As we reeled from the shock, both of us focused on Shirley's family history. Except for her mother, all her blood relatives had died of some form of cancer. As she once said jokingly, "Our family grows things."

The test results forced us to face the ordeal that my wife's cancer might already be systemic. For nearly a week, a fearful numbness prevented my saying much. This was my wife, whom I loved dearly, and I couldn't face the possibility of losing her. Fear so gripped me that I couldn't talk about what lay ahead.

This was the second time in our life together that we had encountered the possibility of impending death. Thirty years earlier, we had been involved in a head-on collision and Shirley's head crashed through the windshield. Doctors had not expected her to survive the night.

All our family members and friends had prayed. Especially important were the prayers of about forty people in the small church where we worshiped. One of them, a man named Gus, spent long hours in prayer. Afterward, he called Shirley's mother and said that God had assured him that Shirley would live. For three days, Shirley's condition didn't change. On the fourth day, the doctor said simply, "There are some things we cannot explain. Everything has been healed." The next day, Shirley walked out of the hospital.

Now, years later, we faced cancer. I prayed for peace, but none came. "I almost lost her once," I cried out to God. "Don't take her. Please don't take her."

Three days before her surgery, I told our pastor, David Fry, about my fear of losing my wife. He urged me to talk with Shirley and tell her how I felt. The next day, Shirley and I sat down, held hands, and together we faced what lay ahead.

We discussed every option about what could happen during the surgery. The doctor might have made a mistake and he would sew up the incision. Perhaps it would be a fairly normal mastectomy and a full recovery. We considered the possibility that she might die during the surgery. The other extreme was that the cancer had become so advanced they would close her up and send her home to die. Tears filled our eyes and our voices cracked when we spoke. We kept on talking because we wanted to be able to accept every possibility and to rejoice together, no matter what happened.

As we talked, my fear slowly dissolved. Shirley arrived at peace long before I did, but by the time we had finished talking, both of us knew that whatever happened would be all right.

She had the mastectomy and the cancer had spread into her lymph nodes. The surgeon removed the nodes and she has been cancer free since September 1999.

I'm writing about this because through that painful experience I learned a valuable lesson about living, about aging, and about dying. In the process of our opening up to each other, both Shirley and I realized on a deep emotional level how deeply we valued our lives and our years together.

> In the process of our opening up to each other, both Shirley and I realized on a deep emotional level how deeply we valued our lives and our years together.

"Life is a gift," Shirley said. "Every day we're alive is an opportunity to give thanks to God."

She said exactly the words I needed to hear. Life is God's special present of love. As I reflect on the events, her words enabled me to appreciate the wonderful gift God had given us.

Since that morning in 1999, every morning I lie in bed a few minutes when I awaken. Over the years I'd done it

> Shirley was right—life is a gift.

spasmodically, but facing life-and-death issues has made me more aware of the great value of the wonderful gift of life. Therefore, I intentionally think of at least ten things for which I'm thankful. Shirley and our life together always head that list. I start every morning with thanksgiving to God for giving us another day on earth together. This continued life isn't something we've earned or are even entitled to. Shirley was right—life is a gift.

As I reflect on aging, I realize that we have no way to appreciate life until we factor in death. We don't value our health until we're sick. We can't fully understand grace until we feel miserable and undeserving. Can we appreciate our possessions unless we've tasted poverty? Is it possible to relish being loved until we also know how it feels to be hated or disliked?

When the day comes—as we know it must—that one of us dies, my hope is that, in the midst of sadness, the one who survives can eventually wipe away tears and say, "Thank you, God, for the gift of life."

Getting older does point toward the end. We can focus on dying, fret about it, worry about the process—and I assume most of us do some of that.

> I have decided that each day is a day for giving thanks. I'm alive and I can enjoy *today.*

I have decided that each day is a day to give thanks. I'm alive and I can enjoy *today.* I can look backward and rejoice that God has been with me each day I've lived.

I appreciate life each day because I've had foretastes of not having life. I've lived long enough to bury my parents, three brothers, and attend the funerals of a number of friends. Recently I read of two pastors I knew and liked— years younger than I am—who died. It saddens me to acknowledge those losses, and yet, I'm thankful. I valued their influence in my life.

As I reflect on the concept of aging, I realize not only is life a gift, but it's also a gift to value and honor. If we take life for granted, it holds little value. Only as we see the contrast of life ending can we pause to thank God for the days we've enjoyed on this earth. If every day is truly a gift, doesn't that also make it easier to surrender life when it's God's time?

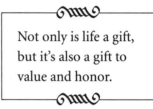

Not only is life a gift, but it's also a gift to value and honor.

The day Shirley went in for surgery, I scrutinized her face. I know her well enough that I would have spotted doubt or fear. There was nothing but peace. "I'm fine," she whispered.

And she was. Even more than I, Shirley valued each day as God's special gift of love. I wonder if that's not the way God wants all of us to appreciate the wonderful treasure he has given us.

As I've talked with others, I've been amazed at how many value their lives, especially as they add years. For instance, only a few months after my writer-friend Yvonne Lehman lost her husband, she wrote these humorous words:

"As you grow older you can look back on your life and see it realistically. You realize the era of girdles did nothing for your stomach fat but push it out on the back and sides of your hips.

> "As you grow older you can look back on your life and see it realistically."

The bleach only made you look cheap but it works now that you're older and the color is closer to your roots (white). The spiked heels gave you a better curve to your calves. But now that you wear only tennis shoes, your calves have fallen with your arches, but so what? You can wear your skirts to your ankles and who cares anyway? Onlookers rarely get past your horn-rimmed, tri-focal eyeglasses, your corduroy skin.

"No matter what you've done to your face, your hair, and your body, it ends up a fallen mess anyway. You end up looking kind of like a jello mold that's turned upside down, splats on the floor, and oozes in whatever shape it so desires. No girdle can contain it.

> "When you stand to sing hymns in church you look at your hand on the back of the pew in front of you and cringe at the chicken-claw look and wonder whatever happened to those graceful, well-formed fingers. Then you stop and thank God that you have hands."

"All the effort that went into staying young, beautiful, and healthy didn't work. You got old anyway and now you accept it and just grin at the young cuties going to all that pain and expense when they're going to end up like you.

"You remember when you began to wave with the 'Miss America' or 'politician wave'? You waved from the wrist because your triceps hung low. You remember when you had a passel of children and wished you had at least three hands instead of two? Now you don't need three because you can keep your two hands where they're needed and wave hello or good-bye with your triceps, and you don't care. All your friends have hanging triceps too—or they will eventually.

"When you stand to sing hymns in church you look at your hand on the back of the pew in front of you and cringe at the chicken-claw look and wonder whatever happened to those graceful, well-formed fingers. Then you stop and thank God that you have hands.

"When young, you feel you have a lifetime ahead of you so you've gotta look good and you've gotta be the best mom, wife, daughter, granddaughter, aunt, neighbor, church member, worker, and the best looking. As you age, you realize you failed and those who thought you were some of that didn't like you because you made them feel inferior. Now you let your warts show, make fun of yourself, and everybody likes you. Besides, you really don't care anymore if they don't. You begin to live your life your way because it gets shorter and shorter. The

> "You used to waste your breath giving your children the benefit of your great wisdom and they never listened. Now they ask for it, but you just laugh and say you don't have any."

way you want to live it is by taking a long nap, getting a good night's sleep, and sleeping in during the morning.

"You no longer think you have to run the church, the PTA, the neighborhood, or the world. You've learned how to say no gracefully. You used to waste your breath giving

> "What it comes down to is that we can try and fix ourselves up, and that ain't bad; but if we failed to fix ourselves up on the inside, we've wasted a lot of time and money."

your children the benefit of your great wisdom and they never listened. Now they ask for it, but you just laugh and say you don't have any.

"The roles have reversed. Your children did listen and now they try to keep a clean house and the beds made, while you no longer bother with those things. It's just a matter of repetition every day and you'd much rather go to the percolator, have a double mocha cappuccino with whipped cream, and laugh with your friends who're in the same boat as you.

"What it comes down to is that we can try and fix ourselves up, and that ain't bad; but if we failed to fix ourselves up on the inside, we've wasted a lot of time and money. What life comes down to is that we're basically alone in the world, and although we should do our best to improve ourselves, what counts in the final analysis is our relationship to the Lord Jesus. The positive side of aging is that you realize it's the quality of life that counts—what we do with the Lord Jesus Christ and how we serve others by serving him."

Yvonne, like a lot of us, finally figured out that God gave us life to enjoy and to laugh about along the way.

Changing

When I lived in Africa, an older missionary constantly called me aside to offer me advice. She prefaced her remarks with "I'm telling you this for your own good." As soon as she said those words, I knew what she really meant was she didn't like the way I did something and she thought her way was better. Sometimes she was correct; more often it was merely a matter of personal preference. She never seemed able to view life objectively. If she saw something that didn't please her, it was wrong. It was right when she liked it.

She frequently tried to change me and others around her. Many people resented her intrusions and I don't think she ever figured out the reason.

> "Be not angry that you cannot make others as you wish them to be, since you cannot make yourself as you wish to be."
> —Thomas à Kempis

I didn't understand it then; I understand it now. When we don't like ourselves, we need to change others. Maturing means we no longer need to change others or to offer advice "for your own good." When we like ourselves, we don't need to fix anyone. Isn't the attempt to change others really a sign that we don't like ourselves? The more I know and accept myself, the more I can accept others as they are. If I'm constantly figuring out plans for others' self-improvement, doesn't that say something about the way I truly understand myself?

I like the way Thomas à Kempis put it: "Be not angry that you cannot make others as you wish them to be, since you cannot make yourself as you wish to be."

> When we don't like ourselves, we need to change others ... When we like ourselves, we don't need to fix anyone. Isn't the attempt to change others really a sign that we don't like ourselves?

We can't change anyone else. The more we try, the more frustrated we become. Too often those who seem the most committed to healing others are showing that they themselves are sick. And as long as we try to correct others or mend their attitudes, we're missing out on the person who needs the most fixing: *ourselves.*

"What a relief to be rid of the burden of being responsible for others' actions," one older friend said. "Focusing on ourselves is empowering. Every day feels more adventurous when we take full responsibility for our thoughts and words, leaving to others what belongs to them."

Many of those I surveyed expressed relief to be rid of the burden of being responsible for others' actions. Concentrating on our own growth empowers us.

Many of us have spent years frustrated, even frantic at times, trying to control the actions and the opinions of others. Accepting that we can't change someone else is the first step toward changing ourselves. And we will change when we stop trying to shape up our friends and instead find new options for our own behavior.

"At this stage of life, I feel more comfortable with who I am," said Rosalie Campbell. "I don't have to meet anyone else's expectations but my own. It's good being me. I'm grateful for my ability to change, even though I feel uncomfortable with some of the feelings that come with new ways. Change means letting go of the old and taking up the new. It means closing doors to methods that opened and kept me in the past and opening the doors of my present reality."

> Many of us have spent years frustrated, even frantic at times, trying to control the actions and the opinions of others. Accepting that we can't change someone else is the first step toward changing ourselves. And we will change when we stop trying to shape up our friends and instead find new options for our own behavior.

Our experiences cause many of us to become rigid in an effort to cling to narrow perceptions of our world. Perhaps it allows us to be safe. It's easier to keep doing what we did in the past instead of going out and trying new things.

> Accepting that we can't change someone else is the first step toward changing ourselves.

The notion of holding everything still and not allowing change may offer security, but it's a restricted life. I have a writer-friend who won't even touch a computer. She has given me a variety of reasons, but I suspect it's her insecurity that keeps her at the typewriter. It's not wrong, but it is safe.

Many of us become rigid in an effort to cling to narrow perceptions of our world and "the way it's supposed to be" (that is, the way it used to be). It's easier and less risky to keep doing what we did in the past instead of going out and trying innovative things or exploring new possibilities.

The nature of life is movement. We're all passing through on a journey. Any ability has really only been temporarily placed in our care by God. When we allow ourselves to let go of the old and make room for the new, we may naively expect life to be easier, more comfortable, and more pleasant.

Maybe it is, but usually not initially. Although we release the old, its voice still haunts us. We tend to want to hold on and beg the world not to change, but life keeps moving. Change brings out anxieties and discomfort.

Here's an example. At one time in my life when work piled up on me, I'd feel overwhelmed, anxious, and would start feeling I could never get everything done. Those feelings all but paralyzed me. Finally, I faced them and the factors behind those feelings (which aren't important to relate here). Then I sat at my desk and wrote a list of all the things I had to accomplish that day. When I saw them, I knew I could do them. "Being overwhelmed is a feeling, not a reality," I said aloud.

For weeks after that, when those old feelings resurfaced, I reminded myself that just because I *felt* overwhelmed, it didn't mean I was. Eventually, those feelings left me. That's when I knew I had truly changed.

> Many of us become rigid in an effort to cling to narrow perceptions of our world and "the way it's supposed to be" (that is, the way it used to be). It's easier and less risky to keep doing what we did in the past instead of going out and trying innovative things or exploring new possibilities.

"Experience keeps me from being too judgmental," said Pastor Bill Patterson. "For instance, if someone fails morally or spiritually, I am more compassionate than I once was. After having counseled with thousands of people, I know the kinds of strong temptations under which people can come. This doesn't mean I am now an enabler, but it means I now understand better how a fault can occur."

Bill's words made me think of Paul's admonition to the Galatians: "Dear friends, if a Christian is overcome by some sin, you who are godly should gently and humbly help that person back onto the right path. And be careful not to fall into the same temptation yourself " (Gal. 6:2 NLT).

There are positive lessons we learn in life only through our own experiences. Once we open ourselves to new experiences, we've already begun to change.

As we become more open to our own needs, we realize the only change we need to be concerned about is in ourselves.

"My grandkids talk to me because I'm their confidant," said Blaine. "Even when I disapprove of something they do, they know I accept them. When my oldest grandson was sixteen, he said, 'Grandpa, you're my best friend. I can tell you anything.'"

Blaine said that, at first, those words shocked him. "Why can't you talk to your parents? They love you," he said.

"They're so uptight over everything," the boy answered. "They're afraid I'm going to do drugs or mess up my life so they're always on my case. They don't listen, they only lecture."

Blaine was old enough and had experienced enough that he was able to see the long road ahead of the boy. The parents, however, saw only the immediate steps. They knew all the pitfalls and detours the boy could take, and they worked hard to change him to what they thought he ought to be. They expended much energy by fretting about what could happen or the slips and falls along the route.

> "Experience keeps me from being too judgmental . . .
> If someone fails morally or spiritually, I am more compassionate than I once was."

One of the things that age does for us is to make us less worried about what would or could happen. We can take the longer view because we've gone down the road ourselves. We know the pitfalls and bumpy spots, but we made it. Now we can guide those who are just beginning the journey.

There are positive lessons we learn in life only through our own experiences. Once we open ourselves to new experiences, we've already begun to change.

Picking up
the Pieces

S omewhere around my early fifties I began to pick
up the discarded pieces of my life—or at least
that's the way I describe it. I began to read about
the mid-life crisis and wondered why I hadn't had one.
According to the literature, it's supposed to hit somewhere in our thirties or forties.

We all make that transition from young to old even
if we don't acknowledge it. Women have a definite
physical transition because of menopause that guides
them into that second stage of life. We males slide more
gradually into the older age. That may be the major
reason that, for some men, hitting mid-life is an
extremely painful process. It's the sudden awareness

that the receding hairline and the increased waist sizes are telling the truth: They're getting older.

Regardless of what we call that shift, it happens. Here's my explanation of the thinking of Carl Gustav Jung, who invented the term *mid-life crisis.* From our youth we're taught to make our way in the world. We focus on moving ahead in the business world, having babies, or getting more education. For us to function, we have to eliminate or ignore parts of ourselves. When that shift in consciousness comes, it's like a ten-foot sign in front of us. We are moving into a new stage of life.

> We all make that transition from young to old even if we don't acknowledge it.

This becomes the denial period for many: They resort to a variety of ways to show the world and prove to themselves that they aren't going downhill. This is when we hear men say, "I'm as strong today as I was when I was thirty." Even they must eventually acknowledge they are no longer the "*now* generation."

As I see it, a healthy way to approach the second half of life is to pause and try to recapture the parts of ourselves that we left behind.

The best way I know to express this is to consider Jung's concepts of the introvert and extrovert. All of us have a preference for one or the other—that's a given. We can function in what we call the inferior mode, but we are at our best when we're true to our basic natures. At mid-life, we tend to go back and pick up the pieces—that is, to incorporate or value those parts of our personality we ignored before.

Another way to say this is that some people are introverts. They're tuned to what's going on inside them and they're inwardly directed. No matter how much advice they receive, they make their final decisions from within.

By contrast, the extroverts are outwardly directed. In both instances I'm thinking of the extreme because most of us are a mixture. Extroverts resonate with people. They lean on others and make decisions based on values and attitudes outside themselves. That's the place where I lived most of my life. I used to say that I didn't even know what I thought about a problem until I talked it over with someone. If I didn't have anyone to talk to, I would write in my journal. I had to understand by throwing the information *out there.*

> A healthy way to approach the second half of life is to pause and try to recapture the parts of ourselves that we left behind.

I used to say I was like the sprinkler system—always throwing out water. That's being outwardly directed.

By contrast, my wife is the classic introvert. Shirley is like the artesian well. By definition, an artesian well is water that goes deep under the ground and then, from internal pressure, flows spontaneously like a fountain. When Shirley confronts a problem, she goes inside. I know where she's starting, but it's as if she goes deeply underground. She's not trying to hide from me, but that's how she processes issues. She may ask my advice before she goes inward, but the decision is totally her own.

So I wait. When she resolves the issue, it's the well that suddenly springs up. I don't know where or when, but the internal pressure eventually forces the solution to the top.

Because my way has been the way of the sprinkler, I had difficulty (and some impatience) with the artesian wells. A friend used to say, "What I see in you is who you are. There's no subterfuge." What I realized is that I made many of my choices by listening to other voices—those I respected—and often endowed them with greater power than I did my own voice.

Somewhere in the aging process, I began to change— slowly—so gradually I wasn't aware of those changes until I had gone down the road quite a distance.

I call that picking up the pieces. By that I mean, as a child I became outwardly directed. As a youngster I was sometimes shy, but I picked up behavioral clues and teachings from "out there." I learned how to dress and behave by connecting with others. I dropped many pieces of my life— and we all do. The more outwardly directed I became, the less my inward nature spoke.

I got along well with people. I'd rather be with a dozen people than to be alone. Even when I started dating Shirley, I took along a couple of friends who didn't have dates.

"Am I dating you or your friends?" Shirley finally asked.

I got the message quickly. After that, it was only the two of us.

Mixed in with this is a powerful biblical principle that I've valued. The purpose of marriage, God said in Genesis 2:24 is for a man and a woman to come together and to "become one."

My understanding of becoming one is that two distinctive personalities blend to form one unified front. Jung said little about marriage, but he did say that introverts tend to marry extroverts. That's the way most good marriages work.

Shirley attracted me in many ways—and most of them were things I didn't realize. She was the quiet one, the listener. She thought issues through and was what I call a deliberate person.

When we lived in Kenya, the Africans watched all of us *wazungu* (foreigners) carefully and secretly gave us names that expressed our character. Shirley overheard Africans talking about us one day and figured out what they were doing. After a great deal of laughing, we learned they had labeled me with the name *Haraka* very early. It's Swahili for *quick, fast.* The Luo people called Shirley *Mos,* which means *slow* or *deliberate.*

The names also implied our basic natures—my being outwardly directed and Shirley inwardly directed.

As I've walked forward on the path of positive aging, not only have I respected introversion more, but I've become tempered and a little less extroverted. That's the way it works when we pause to pick up the pieces. That wasn't a deliberate choice—and I don't think it is with most of us. It's simply the next stage in our aging process—we go back and pick up the pieces of our lives that we previously ignored or left behind.

When we marry or fall in love, we're attracted to those who have qualities we lack. This is just as true in friendship as marriage. David Morgan, my best friend, is an introvert. That may be why we have such a great relationship. He's aware of pushing away extroverted tendencies in his past, just as I'm aware of running away from introverted qualities. We're both quick to admit that we're enjoying the growing—of influencing each other and learning to pick up the pieces.

As I've looked back, I've attracted far more introverts to me than extroverts. That's just how it works. Those who have what we lack attract us. But that's not the end.

Positive erosion gradually takes place. If we follow the normal patterns, the introverts open a little more toward the outside world and the extroverts learn to look inward for direction. That's what good partners and friends do for each other.

> Positive erosion gradually takes place. If we follow the normal patterns, the introverts open a little more toward the outside world and the extroverts learn to look inward for direction. That's what good partners and friends do for each other.

That's also part of picking up the pieces. If I had been left to myself, I probably wouldn't have learned to go inward. For me, my wife and friends have enabled me to pick up those pieces.

As I age, I increasingly feel contented to spend time alone; I enjoy reading more than I ever have; I can sit and think my thoughts and not wonder who I can call to figure out what I'm thinking. I'm starting to make decisions after looking inward and without getting a consensus from others.

Here's one problem we have in picking up the pieces: Our lives are already full. I don't have any space to squeeze in something more—who does? That's where I see the real crisis coming in.

The best way I can explain this is to repeat a story my friend David Morgan told me. A very learned man wanted to become more spiritual so he went to a reputedly wise and godly man. He explained all the things he had learned—and talked for quite a time.

Finally the wise man offered his guest a cup of tea.

"I'd love one," the man said.

The holy man started pouring the tea but he didn't stop. The cup filled and spilled over into the saucer, but he continued to pour. The tea spilled over the sides and fell to the floor.

The guest stared in amazement.

"This is your problem," the holy man said. "You are so full there is no space for anything new. You need to empty yourself of old things to allow the new to enter."

> Here's one problem we have in picking up the pieces: Our lives are already full. I don't have any space to squeeze in something more— who does?

Isn't that how it works? Only as we lay aside certain things can we make room for the new. It's like my boyhood friend Chuck Pekios told me. He had gone to several of our five-year high school reunions. After the thirtieth, he said, "The first few we talked about all our accomplishments and where we were going in our careers. But after thirty years of being out of high school, we didn't need to prove anything to anyone. We were more settled and content."

Isn't that part of picking up the pieces? For some of us, it means we no longer have to prove that we're successful or that we haven't wasted our lives.

That's one of the significant things about picking up the pieces. We can go back and open ourselves to what we bypassed in our hurrying to make our way in the world. But it also means releasing things we no longer need.

I didn't say, "giving up," because that's not how it works. It's releasing—letting go of the things we don't need any longer.

Shortly before a pastor-friend prepared to retire at age sixty-five, he said to me, "I'm not even sure who I am. I've been a pastor since I was twenty-three. That's the only way I know how to relate to people."

Isn't that just as true as the fifty-year-old mother who waves good-bye to her last child? She has to redefine herself. That's not always easy, but it is necessary. As we grow older, we need to seek what fulfills us at this stage of our lives. Motherhood may have

> That's one of the significant things about picking up the pieces. We can go back and open ourselves to what we bypassed in our hurrying to make our way in the world. But it also means releasing things we no longer need.

> We've spent the first half learning and accumulating knowledge. In the second half, we pay more attention to experiencing as opposed to having things . . . Meaning is not the same as learning or accumulating. Living and reflecting on our lives make it exciting.

been wonderful, but who is she now? What about the vibrant athletes who can't do at fifty-five what they did at twenty-five?

Sometime we have to start picking up the pieces. We've spent the first half learning and accumulating knowledge. In the second half, we pay more attention to experiencing as opposed to having things. We realize that meaning is not the same as learning or accumulating. Living and reflecting on our lives make it exciting.

Embracing the aging process makes life more meaningful. In the early stages of picking up those pieces, cultural clichés can make us fear we're losing something. This is what I call self-fulfilling negativity—constantly looking backward and thinking of what we've lost instead of looking around at what we've gained. If we persist, we realize that life becomes richer.

> This is what I call self-fulfilling negativity—constantly looking backward and thinking of what we've lost instead of looking around at what we've gained. If we persist, we realize that life becomes richer.

So I'm picking up the pieces. I still like people and love being with friends and socializing. That's the strong part of me. The growing part of my life—the part that's emerging as I age—is the part that's learning to embrace the inner world as well. I'm less social than I used to be, and I'm comfortable with that.

As I ponder the matter of picking up pieces, I also realize another axiom of people like Jung. He said that we're all moving toward wholeness—to be a whole person.

If that's true—and I believe it is—it means that I'm now adjusting the course of my life. I'm enjoying the richness of the inner life as it merges with the outer. I like who I am as I gaze inward, and I like my place in the world as I gaze outward.

As I continue to pick up the pieces, this is part of the aging process. Or maybe it's better to call it simply another phase of the growing process.

Picking up the Pieces = Changing as we grow older. Making us whole. Moving toward wholeness.

Experiencing instead of Accumulating. Understanding meaning rather and appreciating it.

Today Be Not All Day

Today be not all day," Eunice Princic used to say to me. She was sixty-three and I was in my late twenties. We served together as missionaries in Africa, and she lived in the same house with us.

The meaningless sentence was a literal translation into English from one tribal dialect she spoke. As she explained, the Africans were saying, "Don't hurry. You have time. It is still today so you can get it done."

It took me at least another thirty years to understand those words. This is a message each of us needs to absorb as we continue to age.

Too many of us go through the first decades of our lives believing that every call demands immediate action.

I like the way Betty Freeman phrased her philosophy: "I don't have to do everything today that I used to think I had to get done." She went on to explain that she had spent so many years of her life rushing that she now realizes how foolish some of it had been.

> Too many of us go through the first decades of our lives believing that every call demands immediate action.

Too many of us go through the first decades of our lives believing that every call demands immediate action. Some do, of course, but many of us never figure out the difference.

For so many years of my life, I followed the American culture that subtly tells us that we're only as good as the results of our lives. That leads to a life of accumulation and ostentation. We can't be content merely to have accumulated, we also have to prove to others what we've done. I don't mean *accumulated* only in the sense of piling up riches. This is just as true of accomplishments.

> Somewhere during the aging journey, the urgent becomes something we can handle the next day or the next week.

We not only feel compelled to accomplish, but we also move in a kind of driven frenzy. Then somewhere during the aging journey, the urgent becomes something we can handle the next day or the next week. In some sense, we become more selfish—or we think that's how others perceive us—because we shift our focus. Instead of being always there for others, for example, we finally realize we need to be around for ourselves.

> The things we thought we had to do just aren't as important as they used to be. What is important is enjoying our lives.

The things we thought we had to do just aren't as important as they used to be. What is important is enjoying our lives.

I think of the *Westminster Catechism,* which is a series of 107 questions. The first reads: "What is the chief end of man?" The answer: "Man's chief end is to glorify God and to enjoy him forever." To glorify and enjoy God translates to me that we love God and enjoy the life given to us as a divine gift.

Perhaps that's part of the wisdom of getting older. As I look back, like Betty Freeman, I used to feel compelled to do everything "right now."

My dad used to say, "Why put off until tomorrow what you can do today?" After I had grown, I changed that and asked, "Why put off until tomorrow what I could have done ten minutes ago?" There is something good about that. People like Betty and I always got things done. No matter how busy we were, we'd find a way to take on one more task. We became the dependable people—those who prided themselves on their accomplishments.

This also feeds into the concept of productivity. Our culture values those who do things. In recent accounts of downsizing, I've talked to men in that predicament.

One of them, Patrick Borders, who is in his mid-thirties, said, "I've had to manufacture accomplishments for myself." He was the partial owner of a dot-com company and voluntarily left to keep the company afloat. His wife returned to teaching to support the family while Patrick learned to be a freelance writer.

"I felt I had to have completed tasks behind me every day or I would sink into minor depression," he said of his first months of being the househusband. Over a period of months, he learned that it's all right not to be productive all the time. "I no longer need an ultimate job to fulfill me."

He made another statement that proved the reality of what he meant: "I don't need an ultimate job to define me." He went on to say that for years he looked at his employment to define himself. "I've discovered new ways to define who I am."

Patrick learned that lesson before he was forty; some people haven't learned the lesson at seventy.

All of us arrive at the answer differently, but ultimately we come down to realizing that it's who we are—truly are in the core of our being—that defines us.

If accomplishments don't define us, what does?

All of us arrive at the answer differently, but ultimately we come down to realizing that it's who we are—truly are in the core of our being—that defines us.

If accomplishments don't define us, what does?

All of us arrive at the answer differently, but ultimately we come down to realizing that it's who we are—truly are in the core of our being—that defines us.

Something else has become quite clear to me. For many years of my service for Christ as a pastor, the emphasis was on giving, serving, and sacrificing for others. That is important—and I don't want to minimize it.

But it also says that the more committed to God we yearn to be, the more we tend to ignore ourselves and serve others. Some of us were spiritually brainwashed to believe that God's pattern is epitomized by the acronym *JOY: Jesus* first, *others* second, and *yourself* last. I can't speak for everyone, but part of my "selfishness" has been to realize that I'm as important as anyone else. I don't have to give myself the leftovers of my energy or my time.

I'll illustrate this. One Sunday morning in Sunday school our lesson was on the will of God and how we pray for it. In a class of forty adults, it amazed me how many of them seemed aghast that I would pray for myself.

> To love our neighbor as ourself implies that we already love ourselves.

"Isn't my life as important as anyone else's?" I asked. Then I read Jesus' words: "The most important commandment is this: 'Hear, O Israel! The Lord our God is the one and only Lord. And you must love the Lord your God with all your heart, all your soul, all your mind, and all your strength.' The second is equally important: 'Love your neighbor as yourself.' No other commandment is greater than these" (Mark 12:29–31 NLT).

The point I made is that to love our neighbor as ourself implies that we already love ourselves. Only as we embrace ourselves and lovingly care for our good can we truly grasp the needs of others.

As Mrs. Princic used to say, "Today be not all day." So we realize that we don't need to squander our energies in getting everything done right now, in being constantly productive, but we can expend our energies in embracing ourselves and enjoying our lives.

We can slow down long enough to look at ourselves and our needs.

Maybe one reason getting older shows is because we move slower. It might be God's loving way to say, "Enjoy the scenery as you drive along."

I thought of that in June of 2003 when I drove from Essex, Ontario, Canada, to Guelph. I had no idea how long it would take, and no one had given me the mileage (or kilometers in Canada). As I drove along, I remember admiring the beautiful countryside. I pulled into the right lane and allowed many vehicles to pass me. I wanted to get to Guelph, but I also realized that I didn't need to rush to arrive. I thought of those words again, "Today be not all day."

As I drove along, it was my way to pull back and think of enjoying the ride instead of focusing only on the destination.

Yes, I thought, that's what positive aging means. We learn to enjoy "the now" instead of looking only toward what lies ahead. It's the old saying of "Stop and smell the roses." Today isn't all day. By driving in the right lane, I figured I reached Guelph about twenty minutes later than if I had driven at top speed. That meant I experienced twenty minutes of enjoying the ride instead of pushing to get to a destination.

Today isn't all day, but today is a day for enjoyment. It's a day to enjoy God—it's also a day to enjoy our lives and appreciate ourselves as God's creations.

Enjoy the journey.

The Worst of Times and the Best of Times

I don't know where else to turn," *Ellen told me. "I'm at the end. If you don't help me, I'll probably take my life." She didn't cry or wring her hands. Ellen looked at me through dead eyes and spoke in a low monotone.

After twenty-three years, her husband had walked out on her. "I have no one. Our son is married and has his own life. I haven't worked since shortly after we married. I have nothing. My life is empty." She was an only child and both her parents were dead.

For at least thirty minutes Ellen recited all the hardships she faced and the loneliness of her life. "This is the worst time in my life," she said.

Before I tell you the end of Ellen's story, I'll share the worst time in my life. I had lived in Kenya less than three months. An African headmaster constantly violated the rules by taking girls from our boarding school into his house. He also allowed other male teachers to do the same. The students were all teenaged girls and believed that whatever a teacher told them to do, they should do. Every year, three or four girls became pregnant and left school in disgrace.

One evening, I stood up to Ephraim, the headmaster. When I confronted him, he and half a dozen day-student boys beat me badly. They poured kerosene all over me—which they emptied from the pressure lamps used to light the classroom. They planned to set me on fire. When they couldn't find a match, they panicked, realized what they were doing, and all of them ran away.

I hobbled the three hundred yards to our house. After Shirley bandaged me, we drove almost an hour to another mission station to talk to senior missionaries.

Instead of compassion or concern, the first thing I heard was, "What did you do to provoke the beating?" I received lectures and admonitions, but of the four missionaries I spoke to, none of them offered encouragement or sympathy.

On the bumpy, rain-swept road going back to our small mission station, I felt absolutely alone. Shirley understood, and I knew she hurt for me, but I felt totally alone. The Africans hated me (or so I felt at the time), and the other missionaries condemned me. It was the worst time in my life.

I've told you two true stories. Here's the ending of both of them. Twenty-two years later, I saw Ellen at a shopping mall. She had moved out of our community and it had been years since I'd heard from her. She told me that she had gone back to college where she completed a master's degree and had been teaching in a middle school in the inner city. "I'm going to retire next year, but I've already arranged to come in three afternoons and teach remedial reading." Her face glowed as she talked for several minutes about her students and their achievements. "I've never been so happy in my life."

We went back to the time she had visited my office and the subsequent visits. "I reached the place in my life," she said, "where I can look back and see that the worst times were really the best times."

At first, her words shocked me. Then she said, "I had never done anything on my own. My parents guided my life from birth until I entered college. I married Jeff during my first year and even though I completed college and worked for three months, I depended on him for everything. When he left me, I had to learn to stand on my own." Her eyes twinkled behind her bifocals. "You know what? That horrible experience turned out to be wonderful. After I got past the pain, I was forced to change, to grow, and to experience a fuller life than I ever would have had with Jeff. It really was—in retrospect—one of the best experiences of my life."

> "I reached the place in my life where I can look back and see that the worst times were really the best times."

After I left Ellen, I reflected on my experience in Africa. At the time of my beating, I wanted to return to the States. I couldn't. I wanted to run away from everyone. I had no place to go. Although I had several other bad experiences during my six years in Africa, I now look back at that period as the most memorable time of my life.

That's one of the positives of aging. Those things that seem so devastating at the time turn out to be the most enriching periods of our lives. After my beating, I changed—not overnight and not easily—but that beating by Africans and rejection by fellow missionaries taught me a reliance on God that I had never grasped before. Although I need other people, I also had to learn to stand alone.

Freud said it better than I could: "One day in retrospect the years of struggle will strike you as the most beautiful."

It comes down to the old saying that what doesn't destroy us makes us stronger. That's true, but those words sound quite heartless. I prefer to think of difficult experiences this way. The periods in our lives when we're not sure if we can survive emotionally are actually gates swinging open so we can enter into a new world.

> "After I got past the pain, I was forced to change, to grow, and to experience a fuller life than I ever would have had . . . It really was—in retrospect—one of the best experiences of my life."

> Those things that seem so devastating at the time turn out to be the most enriching periods of our lives.

If there is truth in the adage about hitting a mule with a two-by-four to get its attention, maybe that's how God works with us. When difficulties strike, we see only the immediate situation. It takes time for us to get true perspective.

Some people still look back at their worst experiences as their worst, but those of us who are growing and who have focused on positive aging know those were the decisive moments for us to change directions.

Paul in the Bible put it like this: "And we know that God causes everything to work together for the good of those who love God and are called according to his purpose" (Rom. 8:28 NLT). Too often, however, Bible readers stop with that verse. Some things don't turn out for what seems to be good. We don't recoup our losses and we never get the jobs we dreamed about.

If we read the next verse, however, we then grasp the intent of Romans 8:28: "For God knew his people in advance, and he chose them to become like his Son . . ."

> The periods in our lives when we're not sure if we can survive emotionally are actually gates swinging open so we can enter into a new world.

(v. 29 NLT). The words aren't to assure us that we'll win every battle. In fact, we may need to lose some—perhaps many—before we grasp God's purpose. The purpose is to make us more like Jesus Christ. When we suffer, are rejected, or feel isolated we may actually be progressing toward becoming more like Jesus Christ.

That fits with Hebrews 5:8: "So even though Jesus was God's Son, he learned obedience from the things he suffered" (NLT).

Part of turning the worst of times into the best of times is that we have to suffer and that hurts. If we can willingly take that pain, learn about ourselves, and use those traumatic periods as steps toward growth, then—and only then—do they become the best of times.

Those words express what I had to learn. True happiness and joy come from within. If we insist on looking to others

> The words aren't to assure us that we'll win every battle. In fact, we may need to lose some—perhaps many—before we grasp God's purpose. The purpose is to make us more like Jesus Christ.

to deliver us, guide us, or make us happy, we'll keep living the same kind of life and going from hurt to hurt. Only when we realize that God's best lessons are those we learn in the solitary places and in the darkness, do we realize that the bad can become the beautiful.

Excluded and Invisible

I like volleyball. Although I've never been a star player, I've held my own in the game. Maybe that's why it hurt that day when the men set up a volleyball game and excluded me.

For several months in Louisville, Kentucky, I had been involved in a men's group that met every other Saturday morning. I soon became one of the guys and felt fully accepted.

Until the day of the volleyball game.

A dozen of us from the group met at *Rich's house. At the end of the meeting, Rich pointed out that he had set up a net, "So why don't we play?" He volunteered as captain of one team and appointed the captain for the other.

Within two minutes, every man had been chosen or assigned to play on a team—everyone that is, except for three of us. We were old men. The players were under forty; the three of us were over fifty.

They didn't intentionally snub us or disregard us, but they excluded us without asking if we wanted to join one team or the other. Actually, I *had* wanted to play, but I realized that I had become invisible to them when it came to volleyball. By default, we became their cheering section.

That exclusion reminded me of something my slightly older friend, *Katherine, had once said to me, "When a woman reaches a certain age, she becomes invisible to men. No matter how alert, active, or even attractive she is they no longer see her."

More than just physical activities, we're excluded from many things—and from some of them we probably choose to separate ourselves. Our clothes are often different, our values sometimes conflict, and we often prefer different forms of entertainment.

> "When a woman reaches a certain age, she becomes invisible to men. No matter how alert, active, or even attractive she is they no longer see her."

Even so, none of us likes being excluded or ignored; it hurts when we feel we are. But it occurs to me that this is part of the way God made the human race. I suspect God intended us to march through life with our chronological peers. That doesn't throw us into rigid categories, but for most of us, our friendships stay within a decade or so of those younger or older. That makes sense to me.

One day I grumbled to myself about not being invited when three of my friends went hiking. We sat at a table for lunch and they discussed the trip in front of me. For twenty minutes I became invisible to them.

As I listened and sipped my iced tea, I thought of an account in the Old Testament. King David had been deposed by his beloved son Absalom. As the story opens, David and his loyal soldiers will have to fight Absalom for the throne. David appoints generals and captains to lead the troops.

> David understood the logic of the arrangement, but I wonder how he *felt* about being excluded.

"The king told his troops, 'I am going out with you.' But his men objected strongly. 'You must not go,' they urged. 'If we have to turn and run—and even if half of us die—it will make no difference to Absalom's troops; they will be looking only for you. You are worth ten thousand of us, and it is better that you stay here in the city and send us help if we need it'" (2 Sam. 18:2–3, NLT).

The biblical account tells us that David agrees. He stands at the gate of the city of Mahanaim and watches the troops march out and they are, of course, successful.

That day at lunch as I thought of that story—and of the many times since—I know David understood the logic of the arrangement, but I wonder how he *felt* about being excluded.

He had become an old man—the very man who had been a fearless warrior and leader of troops since his late teens. Now he has been excluded. He's the king and more valuable by staying in a safe place.

That may have been the reason. I suspect there was an even more compelling one: For them, David had passed his prime as their warrior-leader. After all, David's value as the king hadn't stopped him from fighting before. It's quite possible that they recognized it was time for the king to put away his armor forever.

"So he [David] stood at the gate of the city as all the divisions of troops passed by" (2 Sam. 18:4 NLT). His heart must have ached. I wonder if he stared at his wrinkled hands and remembered the time he had killed Goliath or rescued captives from the Amalakites.

That simple incident says to me there comes a time when we move into a new position—when we're excluded by age or ability and we need to recognize that younger and more able people take our place. We don't have to feel inferior. Part of our transition in positive aging is to accept where we are. We don't have to appear younger, try to act more robust than we are, or project any image of what we'd like people to think of us as—we only need to be who we are.

We have our victories behind us—and in our hearts. We don't have to apologize for where we've been or where we can no longer go.

I observed this at a recent Thanksgiving celebration when our kids discussed music. They're in their forties, and they still enjoy the old rock-and-roll music. Brett, my thirteen-year-old grandson, said quietly, "I like rap." I didn't say anything, but I have a number of CDs from the big band era.

If I had spent days listening to rap or rock and roll before our time together, perhaps I could have discussed their music with them.

> What if God intended it that way? Is it possible that God wants us to learn to exclude ourselves and walk beside our peers? It may be a good thing to admit that we have graduated to another level.

> Maybe we need to teach people how to treat us.

As I listened to them, however, I thought the variances of music taste made sense. They were relating to the music of their generation. Their interests reflected their peers and their attitudes. I was entitled to my music as much as they were to theirs. None of them called me outdated, old-fashioned, or boring. They recognized that their tastes differed.

What if God intended it that way? Is it possible that God wants us to learn to exclude ourselves and walk beside our peers? It may be a good thing to admit that we have graduated to another level. Problems and frustrations arise when we insist on being part of the volleyball game and can't keep up with the thirty-year-olds.

In a 2003 film called *Something's Gotta Give,* Jack Nicholson plays (and looks like) a sixty-three-year-old lothario who chases women under thirty and has never been out with a woman over a "certain age." He seems to have the younger ones fall over him and has a date every night with women young enough to be his granddaughters.

After seeing the film, a thirty-something woman friend remarked, "That may sound like a big deal for a man, but as a woman, I wouldn't want to be seen going out with a man that old. What would we have in common?"

Before the film ends, Nicholson finally realizes he is an older man and falls for a fifty-something woman. In the final scene, he plays with his wife's first grandchild. That's where he belongs.

Assuming we're all not like the major character in that film and also assuming we're accepting ourselves as we are, what then? Maybe we need to teach people how to treat us. If we show them grouchy, complaining personalities and talk about the irrelevant past and the way things "are supposed to be" (according to our viewpoints) why would they want to be around us? If we show them that although our faces have wrinkled, and our muscles are less flexible, our minds still work, maybe we can show them that we have things to offer. We might also enable them to realize they don't have the maturity or insight to be one of us. Wouldn't it be exciting if we could encourage the younger generation to anticipate that the next decade of aging is something to look forward to? What would it be like if they yearned to be sixty just as much as they longed to be twenty when they were in their teens?

> Wouldn't it be exciting if we could encourage the younger generation to anticipate that the next decade of aging is something to look forward to? What would it be like if they yearned to be sixty just as much as they longed to be twenty when they were in their teens?

135

What if we show them that the next decades aren't the worst period of life? What if we lived in such a way that they saw every decade is as significant as any other?

As I've stressed throughout this book, we older folks need make no apology. We are who we've become. We have things to teach, and part of that is to show people how we want them to relate to us.

> We older folks need make no apology. We are who we've become. We have things to teach, and part of that is to show people how we want them to relate to us.

During the time I was working on this chapter, I spoke to Bernie Kida, who joined our Sunday school class the summer of 2003. Our class has a wide range of ages and a third of the fifty or so members are over sixty.

Here's what Bernie told me. "My initial hesitation on joining your class was that I wondered if I would really fit in. I had made the incorrect assumption that since the average age of your class was higher than in previous Sunday school classes I've attended, the prevailing thinking would be traditional, compliant, and perhaps, staid.

"I found my assumption to be quite wrong as I have discovered the individuals in class to be rambunctious, full of mischief, and quite like myself—ever questioning. On the contrary, I have found the individuals closer to my age fall on the conservative side of thinking. That realization in and of itself has made my time in your class worthwhile, not to take anything away from your teaching of course. Your thought-provoking questions stir debate and generate opinions. At forty-two I realize that I have so much more in common with Dot Baker and Pat Fields [both in their seventies], than I have with those my age. In essence, I have learned who I would like to emulate should I be fortunate enough to reach such an age.

"One other comment I have is that I see a larger cross section in age in your class than in others, which is a testimony to the broad appeal of your class. I can't think of a healthier combination for spirited discussion."

Is it possible that many of those who are younger have missed out on something? Could it be that because they have thought of those older as outdated and ancient they might make wrong assumptions just as Bernie did?

> "I found my assumption to be quite wrong as I have discovered the individuals in class to be rambunctious, full of mischief, and quite like myself— ever questioning."

If that's correct, maybe we need to teach people how to treat us. And they'll learn if we're willing to show them. We show them best by being who we are.

Handling Problems

I was in my early forties when my alcoholic father died. I flew from Atlanta to Iowa for the funeral. That afternoon, shortly after the funeral, we learned that my older brother Ray had died. He had battled lung cancer for a number of months. We knew he would die, but it shocked all of us that it happened on the day of Dad's funeral. We reeled from the double blow in the same week.

Ray's widow called with the news and one of my sisters passed on the information to us siblings. For several minutes, the remaining six of us stood in my parent's living room and discussed how to tell our mother.

"This news will kill Mom," one sister said.

"She's still in deep grief over losing Dad; what will this do to her?" my youngest brother asked.

As we discussed how to handle the situation, I had a moment of insight—so obvious that I wondered why I hadn't thought of it before or one of my siblings hadn't mentioned it. "How do you think Mom got to be this old? She's handled tragedy and heartaches before."

> "How do you think Mom got to be this old? She's handled tragedy and heartaches before."

"Then you tell her," my sister Wanda said.

I agreed to talk to her. Mom was alone in the kitchen drinking a cup of coffee. I sat down next to her, took her free hand, and said, "Ray died this morning."

Mom's dark eyes peered at me through her thick glasses. Her lips trembled slightly, and tears formed in the corner of her eyes, but she didn't say anything, and let me give her all the details.

After I stopped talking, she said nothing for perhaps a full minute. The slight nodding of her head made me aware that she was processing what she had heard. Finally, she asked, "When is the funeral?"

After I told her, she took one final sip of coffee and pushed the cup away. Slowly she got up from the table, walked past me, down the hallway, into her bedroom, and shut the door. At least an hour later, she came out of her room and asked us if we wanted any of the food friends and neighbors had brought to the house. She hurried into the kitchen to heat up a meal for us.

My mother wasn't the kind of woman to put on a brave front. If she needed to cry, she would cry. That day, she didn't cry in front of us, although her puffy face evidenced that she had done a great deal of it in private.

We remarked among ourselves that Mom handled Ray's death better than the rest of us did. She was seventy-nine years old.

I realized that day—as I never had before—how differently we handle hardships and problems at different ages.

The others went into the kitchen with her and I heard their nervous attempts to sound normal. None of them talked about Ray. From the other room, I could see Mom passing dishes of food around the table.

I thought about the times when I lived there that I had faced what seemed like insurmountable obstacles. We had barely moved into the house when Lois, my first true love, dropped me. She not only broke up with me, but she also started to date my best friend. I didn't think I'd ever get over the pain. Of course, I was seventeen, and it was a catastrophic event.

> I like the philosophy of an older friend who said his favorite words in the Bible (King James Version) were: "And it came to pass." To him, these words meant that all troubles don't have to stay. Thank God, they come to pass.

From there, my mind flipped to other times and other places. I could catalogue heartbreaks and what seemed at the time as insurmountable problems, but I lived through them. I survived and grew stronger as a result of all the conflicts.

By contrast, this morning as I dressed to go outside at

5:30 and run ins the cold, I reflected on how little I worry about anything. Situations that would have upset me at twenty-five or forty don't bother me now. I like the philosophy of an older friend who said his favorite words in the Bible (King James Version) were: "And it came to pass." To him, these words meant that all troubles don't have to stay. Thank God, they come to pass.

He was right, of course, because age gives perspective. We've put mileage on our bodies and years of experiences on our emotions, so we're able to view the long-term effect, instead of seeing everything as an immediate need or an emergency.

Age incorporates experience and calmness in handling tragedies. Every bump in the road is no longer a crisis. It's as if we say, "I've been here before. I can survive this."

This shows up in every area of our lives. For instance, James Tate (age seventy-five) said, "It seems to me that aging has allowed me to be more at peace behind the wheel of my car. In my younger days I angered (intensely) when someone abused 'my territory' on the road. Being an aggressive driver myself, I felt affronted when someone cut me off or tailgated or honked unnecessarily at my driving. Now, I can sit back and smile, wave them by, or accommodate them without the slightest feeling of loss. I usually get where I'm going on time without worrying

> Age gives perspective. Because we've put mileage on our bodies and years of experiences on our emotions, we're able to view the long-term effect.

> Problems and hard-
> ships teach me. I
> don't welcome them,
> but I accept them as
> God's learning tools.

over whether I missed a green light. So this has been my indication of arriving at an older and wiser age."

"The most positive thing about aging is seeing the world as less a crisis than a flow of positive experiences," wrote James Kern. "Things that once seemed so immediately pressing now take on an air of 'we'll work through this as we've worked through so many other things.' This attitude then lends a sense of calm around me and those with whom I share this journey. I like the calm. I enjoy the quiet times. God has provided me a strong body so that even at this age I can enjoy the very active and busy things too. I see no need to change anything in my life right now, and finally, I know that if I perceived a need to change something, I'm free. I can change if I choose to." James is sixty-six.

I doubt that I'll ever get to the place where I never encounter problems. In fact, I hope I don't. Problems and hardships teach me. I don't welcome them, but I accept them as God's learning tools. That idea would never have occurred to me at age fifteen. By thirty-five I "knew" the principle— at least I gave mental assent. By fifty I was able to say, "Yes, I'm beginning to understand."

As I continue to grow older, I not only see difficulties as instructors, but also as absolutely necessary for my contin-ued development.

The difference is that I'm no longer overwhelmed as I was in earlier times. I can pause as I continue my trek up the mountain trail, look back, and remember the trauma and the pain on the way up. Then I smile. "I've made it past all those treacherous and dangerous places. I can make it to the end."

Like my friend, I've finally developed the ability to look at the quandaries, "And it came to pass."

Stuck at an Age

* B en and I met in college, but we weren't particularly good friends. About ten years ago, Ben attempted to contact every member of our freshman class and started corresponding with us. For a long time he mailed us a quarterly letter about various classmates. Last year, he switched to e-mail and I hear from him every month.

In his latest e-mail his first paragraph began, "Those college days were the best years of our lives, weren't they?"

"They were?" I asked aloud. *The best years of our lives?* I didn't like Ben speaking for me, although my college days weren't bad (I liked college very much and graduate school even more), but I could list at least several periods of my life that I consider far more significant.

I've thought quite a bit about Ben and I think he's a man who's been stuck at the age of twenty—the age he was when we met. I didn't know much about the rest of Ben's life until he began to contact me again. My sense is that as far as he's concerned nothing noteworthy happened after his years in college. Or perhaps it's that he never progressed beyond age twenty.

> "Those college days were the best years of our lives, weren't they?"
> "They were?" I asked aloud.

By contrast, I love the comment made by Nobel Prize winner Pearl S. Buck: "Would I wish to be 'young' again? No, for I have learned too much to wish to lose it. It would be like failing to pass a grade in school. I have reached an honorable position in life, because I am old and no longer young. I am a far more valuable person today than I was 50 years ago, or 40 years ago, or 30, 20, or even 10. I HAVE LEARNED SO MUCH SINCE I WAS 70 . . . This, I suppose is because I have perfected my techniques, so that I no longer waste time in learning how to do what I have to do."[5]

I've thought a great deal about Ben, and he fits a theory my friend David Morgan has developed. He speaks of *arrested development*. David built his idea on the work of Erik Erikson who taught that we grow through various stages but that each stage has an optimal time. We can't push children into adulthood (although some parents try), and we can't slow the pace to protect our children from life's demands. God sets a time for each task. If we manage a stage well, we carry away certain virtues and strengths that help us through the next stage.

David theorizes that for some people, a traumatic event happens in their lives. They can't progress, and it freezes their emotional development. Usually, it's something overpoweringly traumatic, but it can also be an extremely positive experience they don't want to release or put behind them.

For instance, Erikson teaches that *identity* precedes *intimacy*. Too often people in our culture strive for emotional closeness with another and it doesn't work because they still don't know who they are. Until they know who they are, they can't establish intimacy with others. They marry and make commitments that fail. Too often they pair up with another individual who also hasn't established a true identity. They didn't establish it together either. Hence, they grow apart.

> For some people, a traumatic event happens in their lives. They can't progress, and it freezes their emotional development.

If David is correct, it means something happens to those individuals and their emotional life goes on hold at that stage of development. That is, they may grow in years but it's as if they throw an anchor into the sea that holds them at that significant time—good or bad.

For example, if I fail in my first attempt at public speaking, I may be terrified of audiences the rest of my life. If my first date is a disaster, that may affect every date I have from then on. If my father rejected me, I may feel rejected by every male.

In 1997, Cliff Harris, who has been drug free for years, told me his story. He was a heroin addict and imprisoned forty-two times before his conversion. The first time he took heroin was so overpowering—absolutely the most marvelous, freeing experience of his life at that point. Every problem disappeared and he felt totally at peace. He became an addict and remained one for twenty years.

"Every time I tried heroin, I was trying to recapture the feeling I experienced the first time," he said. He shook his head and said, "It took me a long time to learn that you never get the first feeling a second time, even if you spend your life trying to get it back."

Here's another example of how this works. Twenty years ago a prominent doctor in our community was convicted of child molestation. I knew the doctor, and although he never discussed his situation with me, he told a mutual friend that he had been raped when he was ten years old. All of the doctor's victims were between the ages of nine and eleven.

That's a terrible situation, and although arrested development isn't always like that, such things happen when we become deeply embarrassed or humiliated. The immature part of us stays stuck there.

> Such things happen when we become deeply embarrassed or humiliated. The immature part of us stays stuck there.

Such people have an age—a period of time—that they've never moved from emotionally. They go on with their lives and they do the normal things, but they're living in the emotional past.

Occasionally I ask people, "When you look into the mirror, how old are you?" Here are three examples of people who gave me answers. The interpretation is conjecture on my part, but I believe they were stuck at a particular age.

First, when *Rose turned fifty, I asked her how she felt. "I feel like I'm twenty-five." I had known Rose since she was a teen, and I said, "Isn't that about how old you were when you were married to Jack?"

After she thought about it, she said, "Yes, I guess that's true." She had married him when she was eighteen and he died in a hunting accident eight years later. Without any prompting from me, she said, "You know, those eight years were the happiest of my entire life."

I understand why she might want to think of herself as twenty-five.

> All three of those people seemed stuck at a particular age. It was as if they had stopped growing emotionally at a certain point. Some people hold on to an age and, in their minds, never get older.

Second, when I was a pastor in my forties, *Oz was in his fifties. We talked about getting older and he said, "When I look in the mirror, I don't see my white hair; I'm blond and twenty-three years old."

I didn't follow up the conversation, but I knew something about his background. I suspect that was the age when his mother dictated his occupation. He became a high school biology teacher for the next thirty years. Even though he was good at what he did, Oz hated his job. He had wanted to be an artist but his mother convinced him to teach, "There's no money in art."

He often spoke of how much he disliked his mother. She was a gossip, highly opinionated, and he nearly always ended by saying, "She always thinks she's right about everything."

Third, at a seniors' dance, from across the room I spotted a woman with a girlish figure and the clothes of a teenager. Her blonde hairdo was what I saw sixteen-year-old girls wearing. When she turned around, I stared at her wrinkled face and dyed-blonde hair. She had to have been at least sixty.

All three of those people seemed stuck at a particular age. It was as if they had stopped growing emotionally at a certain point. Some people hold on to an age and, in their minds, never get older.

I'm not trying to play judge or detective, but many people do live at one age in life and never move on. They're stuck and regardless of what the calendar says, they don't move on.

The best illustration I can offer appears in Charles Dickens's *Great Expectations*. Pip, the hero of the book, visits the rundown mansion of Miss Havisham. Dickens devotes a long space to describe the room.

> . . . It was spacious, and I dare say had once been handsome, but every discernible thing in it was covered with dust and mould, and dropping to pieces. The most prominent object was a long table with a table-cloth spread on it, as if a feast had been in preparation when the house and the clocks all stopped together. An èpergne or centre-piece of some kind was in the middle of this cloth; it was so heavily overhung with cobwebs that its form was quite undistinguishable . . .[6]

Miss Havisham's fiancé had jilted her just before the wedding (although we don't learn details until later). She points to a heap of cobwebs in the center of the table:

> "What do you think that is?" she asked me, again pointing with her stick; "that, where the cobwebs are?"
> "I can't guess what it is, ma'am."
> "It's a great cake. A bride-cake. Mine!"[7]

After being jilted Miss Havisham turns against all men. Throughout the rest of the book, readers realize that her life was arrested on the day of her rejection.

If we see ourselves as thirty-four or forty-eight, it holds us back from the flow of natural progression.

By contrast, I've met people who retain a youthful, adventuresome spirit all their lives. Years ago I wrote the autobiography of Norman Vaughan who had gone to the South Pole with Admiral Byrd in 1928.[8]

The last time I saw Norman he was ninety-four years old and had only recently climbed a mountain in Antarctica that Byrd had named for him—and a mountain that no one had ever scaled.

What I liked about Norman from the time I met him was that, despite the years on his body, his spirit remained alive. He loved adventure and constantly saw new things. He wasn't a man who lived in the past. His present was too exciting.

What do we do if we discover we're stuck at an age? The only answer I know is that we have to progress through certain stages. If we don't, we have to go back and pick up where we stopped. To get unstuck may require professional help. It certainly won't be easy to change, but it will be worthwhile.

If we're stuck "back there" someplace, we can't be emotionally open to today. We can't anticipate a greater future because the past still chains us.

Who of us wants to finish life like Miss Havisham? Her emotional life stopped on one sad, disappointing day. That, in itself, is tragic, but the greater tragedy is that she also ruined the life of her ward Estella by turning her against Pip and all men.

> To get unstuck may require professional help. It certainly won't be easy to change, but it will be worthwhile.

Most of the people who responded to my original question about positive aging gave strong evidence of growing and moving on. They smiled at the future, even though they might have had regrets about choices they made in the past.

My favorite answer to the question came from Pat Fields. "Seventy-eight. That's my age now. That's who I like being."

If you knew Pat, you'd understand. She has physical problems and she's had several surgeries in recent years. Her body is going downhill, but her spirit continues to soar. That woman isn't stuck at any age.

Time for Me

M y wife and I have raised five children, served on almost every committee in the church and in the public schools. I'm now into my fifties and still in the workforce, but I'm enjoying not being part of every activity that asks for volunteers," said Ralph Simmons. "This is time for me. I've become more centered on myself. I'm reading books and attending lectures on self-growth. I like myself a lot more now than I ever did before. Doris and I are free to explore and do our thing—no matter what it is. We took a Caribbean Cruise last year. This year, we've decided to spend my three weeks of vacation to visit friends from my high school and college days in five different states. This is selfish, I tell myself, and then I smile and say, 'Yep, and it's about time.'"

This is typical of responses I've received from people.

Here's another.

"When anyone asks me how I feel I say, 'Excellent, considering' and then don't say anything more." *Jenny is in good health and swims three times a week at the YWCA.

"Why do you say that?" I asked.

"It's a wonderful excuse to say no to anything I don't want to do. If I were the more forthright type, maybe I wouldn't need to hide behind my age, but this works for me. My blood pressure is just high enough for me to take medication. My friends know of 'my condition,' although I confess I let them think it's worse than it actually is."

"This is selfish, I tell myself, and then I smile and say, 'Yep, and it's about time.'"

That is her way of making time for herself. Jenny is one of those sweet, kind individuals who never learned to say no. Now she's discovered a way to do it. "I like having time to do what I want to do," she added.

Here's the response from *Melody. She had worked for the same company and in the same department since she graduated from college until she was fifty-four years old. Finally, she realized how much she hated her job—although it paid well. When the company offered early-retirement inducements, she grabbed the opportunity and waved good-bye.

Her two children were grown, married, and didn't need her. Her husband of twenty-seven years had gotten involved with a younger woman and left her two years earlier. The first thing she did was promise herself to do all the things she hadn't done before.

Every week for one full year she vowed to herself to do one new thing. "I couldn't have done that before, but now I was free and no one depended on me. I visited museums, went to live theater, drove to a mountain and did a one-day hike alone. I had my first body massage during my ninth week. In my fifteenth week, I joined a literary discussion group and actually read more than a dozen books. I went up in a hot-air balloon in my twentieth week.

"Somewhere around the twenty-sixth week I decided to go back to church—something I had drifted away from in my thirties. To my surprise, I discovered renewed peace from God and welcoming warmth through the arms of God's people. The next week I visited a Sunday school class. On my thirtieth week I went on a women's retreat and committed my life to God's service. My last adventure was a trip to Nicaragua with a church group. We built a house for a pastor—and I was a woman who said she couldn't even hit a nail straight."

> Melody had learned something important—she had learned to take time for herself.

Melody had learned something important—she had learned to take time for herself. For her, this stage of life is a time to rise above traditional responsibilities. "I don't worry about others like I used to," she said.

Time for ourselves can be a period of self-discovery or an opportunity for couples to get to know each other again. "My husband and I still loved each other, but we'd lost contact with each other," one woman wrote. "Between his career and my being a homemaker with three kids, we had drifted apart. Both of us wanted to rekindle that relationship."

Shirley and I hadn't drifted, but when our third child left home, it was a special, wonderful time for us. We no longer had to make plans for the kids or wonder if they could manage on their own. We traveled together to Europe several times, visited the Holy Land, took ballroom dancing lessons, and visited restaurants that we felt we couldn't afford when the kids were home.

> "My face is more relaxed, my blood pressure is down, and I enjoy life much more. Every morning, I pause to thank God for setting me free to enjoy the good life that God has prepared for us."

"The feeling of freedom comes from being who I really am," Marty Nelson said. He admitted that he no longer attempts to be the dashing hero hunk who used to walk along the beach and display his bulging muscles to young women. "I learned that being my age is freer because I let myself *feel* free. For a long time, I tried to look thirty-five by letting my hair grow longer and combing it over the bald spots. One day I realized that as long as I denied my age, I wasn't free."

Marty went on to say that for years he had avoided conversation that might point to his age. "I became adept at shifting the topic of conversation just before it became uncomfortable. I wanted people to believe I was at least ten years younger than I was. Now I go out of my way to mention that I was in Vietnam, I sing the songs of the Beatles, and

I still play Simon and Garfunkel music. I'm no longer embarrassed that people know my age. I like it better when they tell me how good I look at age fifty-nine. My face is more relaxed, my blood pressure is down, and I enjoy life much more. Every morning, I pause to thank God for setting me free to enjoy the good life that God has prepared for us."

As I thought about the concept of time for me, I realized how it came about. Two factors enabled me to lighten up and to enjoy my life. First, I've worked hard my adult life. Shirley and I have chosen to live a simple lifestyle, regardless of our income. We've been able to put aside retirement money.

Second, one day my friend David said exactly the right thing to me. We had just moved back to Atlanta in 1992. He talked about what I had done with my life and said, "Now you can enjoy your success."

> Just those simple words changed my attitude: "You can enjoy your success."

Just those simple words changed my attitude: "You can enjoy your success." As I pondered those words over the next few days, I thought of so many people who had worked hard and died without enjoying what they had worked toward.

I decided that I would work a little less and enjoy life a lot more, so I gave myself a gift—I decided to become a gardener. My dad had been a farmer until he lost everything in what we call the Great Depression. I think I inherited a green thumb from him. However, he made me work so hard as a kid, I never wanted to plant or weed again.

In 1992, we bought our current house, the former owners had planted a few flowers but it was mostly grass. At least once a week I cranked up the lawnmower and cut the three-quarters of an acre of grass.

The second spring, I stared at the yard and heard myself say, "Grass is boring." I decided to plant flowers and ground cover in front. The next year I tackled a little more of the yard. Today, my yard contains no grass—only flowers, shrubs, and ground cover.

I've enjoyed this and it has truly been time for me. From late March until the end of September, I shut off my computer by five in the afternoon and I change into old clothes and get down on my hands and knees. I tell my friends that every afternoon I play in the yard. It is play.

I wish Dad were alive so I could explain how it feels for my fingers to caress a leaf or for me to smell the fresh dirt. Many afternoons I rush into the house and beg Shirley to come to the door to show her which blooms have opened.

> No matter how stressful my day has been, when I'm outside playing for an hour or two, I feel energized. I appreciate my world and the wonderful gift of life.

This is time for me. I empty my mind of concerns and play. I pray a little, I sing a lot, and love to stare in amazement at the plants as they poke their heads above the ground.

No matter how stressful my day has been, when I'm outside playing for an hour or two, I feel energized. I appreciate my world and the wonderful gift of life.

Something else I've learned about devoting more time for me. The more time I spend with me, the less time I focus on getting other people straightened out. I've become more accepting of myself and that enables me to accept others. I'm also less critical of others' lifestyles and choices. The more I like me, the more I like others and enjoy them. I've gained tremendously more self-confidence in the last few years. I've become more integrated as a person, more willing to trust my instincts (my hunches). My work has become more daring and I'm willing to take chances.

In 1998, Susan Titus Osborn invited me to go to India to teach writing in three different locations in the country. We would have to pay our own expenses to go, but the Indians would take care of us while we were inside the country. I enthusiastically agreed.

> Something else I've learned about devoting more time for me. The more time I spend with me, the less time I focus on getting other people straightened out. I've become more accepting of myself and that enables me to accept others.

After I spread the word of my travel plans, a friend twelve years my junior urged me not to travel to India. He pointed out the poverty, disease, and the growing anti-American feeling in developing nations. He ended with, "Besides, you're too old to do this."

"I'm too young not to do this," I answered.

I went. I loved it. Susan and I had a wonderful adventure. The following year I went back for three weeks with my writer-friend, Jim Watkins.

Both times I was gone for twenty-three days. That's almost a month when I couldn't do my own work. The only times I saw a computer were the three times in Hyderabad when we were able to log on for e-mail.

Did I miss my writing? Did I think about the unfinished manuscript that was due four weeks after my return? To my surprise, the answer was no. I was enjoying myself too much. It was time for me.

More-so Attitude

I first heard about the more-so attitude after I had been a pastor for about three years. I regularly visited an elderly woman named *Mary. She wasn't pleasant to visit. Each time, I sat quietly (she gave me little opportunity to speak) while she went into a litany of complaints about her doctors, neighbors, and her children. She always saved the church people for last and seemed to relish in telling me about the hypocrisy of our elders.

One day as I was leaving her house, her neighbor Henry must have seen the dejected look on my face. He came out of his house, greeted me, and said, "Come on inside for a cup of coffee. After listening to her for half an hour, I'll bet you need something to make you feel like a worthwhile human being again."

I refused the coffee and said something like, "I thought elderly people were supposed to be sweet and kind."

Henry laughed. "It doesn't work that way. It's the principle of 'more so.'" He must have seen the puzzled expression on my face. "What you are when you're young, you become more so when you get older." He and Mary were approximately the same age and had known each other since they were children. "She's the same sad, unhappy person she's always been." He shook his head and added, "Only more so."

> "It's the principle of 'more so.' What you are when you're young, you become more-so when you get older."

Our basic personalities persist throughout our life span. Mary had always been unhappy. Just because her hair had turned white, she didn't become a cuddly sweet grandmother. Shortly afterward, she moved into a step-down care facility, made life miserable for everyone around her, and died a few months later.

Mary was who she'd always been—only more so.

Over the years, I've thought about this principle when I've met individuals. The irascible and cantankerous don't punch a button at age forty-nine and become gentle and pleasant. The sweet, jolly grandfather didn't become that way overnight—he was showing the result of a lifestyle.

This leads me to believe that the most essential determinant of successful aging is our attitude. Each of us has the difficult task of steering our own ship through the challenging

> The most essential determinant of successful aging is our attitude.

waters of life, but we set that course quite early. I believe people can change—but they don't change much.

Here's an example. *Billy and I have known each other since we were in third grade—it was the kind of friendship that flourished and declined through the next decade. The summer I graduated from high school, we did a lot of things together and double-dated often.

I left home at eighteen. Billy and I never saw each other again for thirty-five years. After we had reunited and slid past, "Do you remember . . . ?" we began to talk about our present lives. We were born the same year and came from fairly much the same economic background.

"I hate my life," Billy said.

I stared at him in amazement as he talked of his boredom and the meaninglessness of existence. He was already on medication for high blood pressure, diabetes, and a heart condition, and he seldom had days when he felt good. His favorite topic was to complain about the lack of morals in our society, and how women were running the workplace and pushing men aside.

> It took me a while to remember that Billy had been a negative type at age thirteen. He was still the same person—only more so.

"I hate my life," he said a second time.

Not very wisely, I said, "I love my life." Although that was true, I stopped Billy's openness. I suspect that I was the only person to whom he had spoken those words. I felt sorry for him and I had been so unready to hear what he said, I didn't handle the situation well.

Billy hates his life? I thought at first, surely not. Hadn't he been one of those robust, athletic types who excelled in football or softball? He was the best math student I ever studied with in junior high school.

> Those of us who choose an attitude of kindness become more so as the years go by. If our attitude is one of discontent, we can expect a more-so ending.

As I pondered that, I also remembered Billy as a loner, because he never got along with people very much. We had been good friends in seventh grade, but he complained about several of the people I liked. It took me awhile to remember that Billy had been a negative type at age thirteen. He was still the same person—only more so.

Many things in life we can't control, but we can navigate through life by the channels we choose. We can adjust our course, but most of us don't make radical changes.

I think of the roads in rural Africa where we lived. The long rains were a difficult time for us. That meant for three months it rained every day, often all night long and throughout the day. When we decided to drive on the red-clay roads, we chose our rut carefully. Once we started, it would be hard to move out of it for perhaps five miles. Isn't that how our personalities work? By our attitude we make choices and eventually our choices take over and form our attitude.

Those of us who choose an attitude of kindness become more so as the years go by. If our attitude is one of discontent, we can expect a more-so ending.

The Bible, however, constantly holds out hope. Three times Jeremiah cries out to the people to change, and the command implies that they can do what God urges: "Thus saith the LORD of hosts, the God of Israel, Amend your ways and your doings, and I will cause you to dwell in this place" (Jeremiah 7:3 KJV). (See also Jeremiah 7:15 and 26:13.)

It reminds me of a friend who talked with David Morgan about anger. Although he was a fairly even-tempered man, he confessed he was afraid of his anger. He came from a home where the father often exploded in violent temper tantrums. "I'm afraid of being like him."

The man was in his fifties and David said, "What makes you think you'll make a drastic change like that? Look at all the years you've lived and not become violent. I've never known you to go into rage. I can understand your fear, but it's not anything I would worry about."

In different words, David was stressing the more-so principle. In the future the friend would be who he was now—only more so.

It may take a drastic action for us to change our ways, but we can. In another book, *The God Who Pursues*,[9] I told about a horrible but life changing experience in Africa. I had been a Christian almost ten years and been as sincere in my commitment and service as I knew how to be. One day, however, God made me realize the depth of my sinful nature. For days I didn't want to leave the house. I felt as if everyone could see the shame and sinfulness imprinted on my face.

That turned out to be one of the most difficult and painful times in my life. I was in a foreign country; I couldn't go back to America, and I had to face myself. I didn't like what I saw. The result is that I had a distinct change of attitude. I hadn't been involved in any deep sin, but I had to face things about myself that I didn't like (and even despised). My attitude changed.

Years later, I look back at that time and realize that, as painful as it was for me, my attitude changed. I'm kinder to people, more open to others, and less judgmental. I made a distinct choice then to change. I'm still the same person only more so.

As I continue to age, I want to be everything I can be—and even more so.

Let's Return Thanks

In the early days after my conversion, I would sometimes be seated with Christians and someone would say, "Let's return thanks." That expression sounded awkward to me. (It still does.)

I asked once what it meant and the raised eyebrow implied my question bordered on the sacrilegious. "It means we thank God for providing for our food," my hostess said and turned away from me.

I didn't respond to her. I understood what was taking place but not the expression. I've come to think of it as a lovely, shorthand way of saying, "I am saying a few words of thanksgiving in appreciation to God for the blessings I've received."

Even though I still don't understand the term, the principle is totally right. I've realized that not everyone can give thanks. Some people expect their lives to be blessed and when theirs isn't, they cry out, "Why me, God?" But if we're genuinely thankful, saying the words (even if we tend to limit the expression to praying over our food) is a good reminder to us to give back something. So I suppose the expression "return thanks" means that in appreciation for God's gifts, our return is that of appreciation.

The older I get and the wider my perspective on life grows, the more thankful I've become. Perhaps true thanksgiving is only for those of us who have aged a bit. It's no longer, "Thank you, Lord," for

> I've realized that not everyone can give thanks. Some people expect their lives to be blessed and when theirs isn't, they cry out, "Why me, God?"

answered prayer or for a promotion or getting chosen on the basketball team. It's an attitude—a lifestyle. Being thankful becomes a way of life for us.

In the pages that follow, I want to share comments by other people as they point out the way of returning thanks to God.

Marion Hill said it well: "I've learned to give thanks each day for the day, because I can see that each day *is* a gift."

For some, giving thanks comes spontaneously; others of us have to work at constant awareness. But whether it's natural or we cultivate it, it's a wonderful habit.

Samantha Landy quoted something she had heard Andy Rooney say: "If an older woman doesn't want to watch the game, she doesn't sit around whining about it. She does something she wants to do. And it's usually something more interesting."

Then she added, "As successful seniors, we have given up whining long ago and started doing something about those things we can change."

"I hear too many whines and complaints about getting older. As if it is inevitable that as we age, we leave bits and pieces in a trail behind us," fifty-four-year-old JoAnn Wray said. "I find that aging has given me freedoms I never dreamed of." She went on to speak of the wonderful blessing and freedom that getting older has been to her.

> "I've learned to give thanks each day for the day, because I can see that each day *is* a gift."

"Knowing the depth of God's loving me just as I am has enabled me to be comfortable with who I am and how people perceive me. Every week someone somewhere walks up to me at the grocery, in the mall, in a restaurant, and suddenly they are telling me their life story. Maybe that's because I remind them of their mom or aunt or granny. That's fine. It's God.

"I get to provide a listening ear, to let them know God cares, and to pray with them. God wants to use me in this role and it's an exciting journey. Almost thirty-five years of a very blessed marriage have taught me that God's love wrapped around a couple indeed ties them with a threefold cord that cannot be broken through every trial in life.

"I'm also better able to see the humorous side of life and share a merry heart with others, even if it means laughing at my own foibles. Ultimately, that means I'm aware that I'm an imperfect human being who is sheltered and showered by the grace of God. When it is about Who we know and not who we are, the road of life ahead becomes one we delight in walking daily. I'm never afraid to tell folks how old I am. It just means I'm one year closer to the mansion He's building for me."

"When I was young, I counted my life in decades. Now that I have grown older, I gladly count my life in sunrises," wrote Clarence Edward Cahill.

Just after the start of the new millennium, HBO aired a special called *A Century of Living* about people who had lived and experienced most of the twentieth century. One woman impressed me more than any of the others. She was a hundred years old, blind, and talked of the many losses and hardships in her life. When she finished, she paused. Tears filled her eyes and a smile covered her face. "Life is so wonderful! I'd like to do it all over again."

> "When I was young, I counted my life in decades. Now that I have grown older, I gladly count my life in sunrises," wrote Clarence Edward Cahill.

Can there be a greater act of thanksgiving than that?

"The experiences of our youth have prepared us to identify the wonderful blessings available each day, and to help us make the best of all opportunities that God has afforded us," said Wiley Sloan. "The experiences of our youth have prepared us to identify all of the wonderful blessings available each day, and to help us make the best of all opportunities that God has afforded us."

"By far the best thing about aging is the perspective we gain from experience. I treasure children and what they say, compared to my liking them in my twenties. I don't mind the messes they make, because now I reach for the camera instead of the broom. I take time for relationships instead of wanting the house to look perfect," Jana Heirent said. "This is why grandchildren are so much more special than our own children were. I had my last child at age forty-two (I'm now fifty), and I am parenting the younger ones differently; I'm enjoying them in a different way than I did in my twenties. Most of all, it's about appreciating relationships."

Here's another response from my friend, Samantha Landy:

"Some years ago, I happened to be standing in front of the sliding, mirrored closet door in my bedroom as I put on my hand lotion. Rubbing the lotion around the cuticles as my mother used to remind me, suddenly I thought, Lord, all of my life I have hated my long fingers and hands. Now that I'm finally keeping them manicured and soft, I see maybe they really are okay. I guess when other people have told me I have pretty hands, it's because I do. I just couldn't see it before now. What other distorted ideas have I had about myself?

"There wasn't an immediate answer, but I did feel strangely warm and loved by my Father as I decided that day to go on a mental journey, checking my self-talk concerning me and my attitudes about myself, my body and who I perceive I am.

"As a child, growing up in a fundamental church, we were taught we must be careful not to get into pride. Parents didn't compliment their children so they wouldn't get prideful, maybe thinking that that would help their self-talk stay positive.

"The self-talk we all have, all of our waking hours, needs to be checked often to see if we are building ourselves up or tearing ourselves down just by our attitude and belief system. Often that belief system is defective, based on critical childhood experiences.

"Now that I'm growing up, I am learning not to allow myself to get into negative self-talk. I'm learning that just because someone rejects us, or doesn't like us, it doesn't mean we are a bad person. Maybe it means people don't like themselves. Or maybe that person feels threatened in some way. In the past, I would never have considered that a possibility. I am learning I am only responsible for my own attitudes and actions.

"I guess the Lord feels he can trust me with learning to feel good about myself, knowing at my advancing age, I probably won't have too much time to get into the sin of pride anymore! Or is it simply that God wants us, at any age, to feel good about the body, talents, attributes, and personality he took time to give us, even before we were born?

> "I'm learning that just because someone rejects us, or doesn't like us, it doesn't mean we are a bad person. Maybe it means people don't like themselves."

"King David wrote about how wonderful we are in Psalm 139:14 when he said, 'I will praise You, for I am fearfully and wonderfully made; marvelous are Your works, and that my soul knows very well' (NKJV). We may not be kings, but the Creator of the Universe has fearfully and wonderfully made us. No matter what our age, he loves us and desires a close relationship with us. That's reason enough to constantly give thanks."

Paying Back

After I had been publishing about three years, I promised God that I would not stop learning and would keep striving to be the best writer I could be with the talent he had given me. I made a second promise that I would do everything I could to help other writers become their best.

I was about forty years old at the time. Those who are familiar with Erik Erikson's eight stages of growth will recognize that as part of stage seven. It's the time when we focus on giving back to the world. In my case, I was so grateful for all that God had done for me in those first three years—including about a hundred articles published and a contract for my first book—that I didn't see my attitude as one of reaching a stage of maturity. It simply seemed natural to me to give back.

I could never repay God; I could pay back in the sense of passing on what I had learned. That's been my attitude and intention since those days. I'm also amazed at those who don't pay back.

Here's a negative example. For ten years I was involved in something we call the men's movement—which predated Promise Keepers by a decade. It was a time where men learned to open up to other men and to become vulnerable to one another. I learned so much from other men. They taught me vulnerability and transparency. They taught me—often by example—that it was all right to feel pain, and especially that I could cry when I hurt.

> I could never repay God; I could pay back in the sense of passing on what I had learned.

I noticed the men who came into our group. Many of them came in as angry, pain-filled, damaged males and after a number of months, they felt healed, and they left. Few of them stayed to pass on what they had learned.

One day I talked to one man who had dropped out. "There's really nothing new for me in the group," he said.

"You gained so much from the others," I said. "You're now at the place where you can become a real elder to the younger men."

As I listened, I understood his position and those of many who left us. They had come in to receive, and they found what they sought. None of them seriously considered staying for the benefit of the new ones.

As he walked away, I felt sad. I remembered the first few times he came and how we had reached out to him and accepted him. He didn't need the group any longer, but he couldn't grasp that others—the still-hurting ones—needed him. He could have mentored them and made their journey much easier.

Increasingly, we talk about mentors and role models in our culture. I wish more of us older adults would see this as

> They had come in to receive, and they found what they sought. None of them seriously considered staying for the benefit of the new ones.

a divinely given privilege. Those of us who have aged enough to take on the responsibility and privilege want to educate and enrich others. I've begun to understand why some adults move into the payback mode and some never seriously give themselves.

"*Mentoring*" is the big word now, and I see it all the time. When we combine mentoring with aging, I think the concept forces us to rethink the concept. Most of the time we think of mentoring in the business world, such as the executive who takes younger employees and guides them through the pitfalls of the company.

Mentoring is a process of linking ourselves as resources to others and empowering them to grow and live more effectively.

I prefer the term *giving back*. I like the implications of the term. Using those two words acknowledges that we have received from others. We have been helped, instructed, shepherded, mentored, discipled, guided—regardless of the label. We are where we are in life partially because someone else cared—and probably a lot of someones.

> Mentoring is a process of linking ourselves as resources to others and empowering them to grow and live more effectively.

Giving back offers a way for us to give thanks to God and indicates the seriousness of our gratitude. I began to use the term *payback* about four years after I started publishing. I was in my forties and began to teach at writers' conferences. I was still climbing the ladder of professionalism, but by teaching those who were still on the rungs below me, I could reach down and give them a hand so they could climb higher.

This fits well into Erik Erikson's thinking in which he outlined eight stages of human growth. The seventh stage he called Middle Adulthood and assumed this took place between the ages of forty and sixty-five. That's not a rigid age line, but a period generally characterized as when adults become actively involved in raising and nurturing children,

> At some point in our growing we ask ourselves, "Will I produce something of real value?" We produce that best by paying back for the blessings we've received.

but it doesn't stop there. He taught that as mature adults go through middle adulthood, they engage in other generative activities such as teaching, mentoring, writing, social activism, producing music, or anything that satisfies the need to be needed by others.

As he did with all the stages, he described it as both negative and positive. It's a time either of generativity or self-absorption and despair.

If we're growing as we're aging, we realize this is the time when we look outside ourselves and care for others. We find ways to satisfy and support the next generation. Regardless of what we've done in our lives or who we are, at some point in our growing, we ask ourselves, "Will I produce something of real value?" We stand a good chance of doing so by paying back for the blessings we've received.

> This is the time when we look outside ourselves and care for others. We find ways to satisfy and support the next generation.

In Erikson's sixth stage, love was a big factor—it was a time to develop loving relationships. There was one difference: Love had to be reciprocated. Generativity moves beyond that—it's still about love but this love gives whether it's reciprocated or not.

We give back because it's the right thing to do and because it's what we need to do—for ourselves and for those who follow us. As one of my friends said, "I want to feel I've made a difference to someone in my life."

"The most positive aspect of aging is mentoring," said Pastor Jon Drury. "Getting older provides the increasingly valuable opportunity to make a significant difference in lives. The older I get, the more I have to share. At the time most seniors reach for the rocking chair is when they have the greatest chance of changing the world."

Jon added, "In the past five years I have mentored probably fifteen men, in one-on-two or one-on-three settings. We have set a program of Scripture memory, Bible study, reading, mutual accountability, and prayer. It is demanding, and

> We give back because it's the right thing to do and because it's what we need to do—for ourselves and for those who follow us.

takes the highest degree of commitment, both from the mentor and the students. I currently mentor two guys in their twenties, both missionary candidates (Brian and Doug), and a guy in his early thirties (Mihail). We meet at 5:30 AM on Thursdays at a donut shop. This current group will run September through May. Apart from my wife, my children, and my grandchildren, this is my most strategic ministry."

Roger Palms said that those born after 1981 are looking for the "gray heads" for the values that the rest of the world is devoid of. "They are searching for proven foundations.

> "At the time most seniors reach for the rocking chair is when they have the greatest chance of changing the world."

"This is true in your family if you have nurtured a loving relationship with your kids, the opportunities get richer. I asked my son if he would like me to pronounce a blessing on our first grandchild, his son Judah. I put together a blessing with some Hebrew and Greek phrases from Scripture, and combined lines from Jacob's blessing of Judah in the Scriptures. It was a meaningful opportunity, and was done at the baby dedication. I will probably pronounce a blessing on our second grandchild after it comes in May."

"The great use of life is to spend it for something that will outlast us," wrote William James.

Lannie Dumont died at age ninety-eight. Her great-grandson said at her funeral, "She was my role model and my mentor." Burt was thirty and said, "When I get that old, I want to be swimming and walking and enjoying my friends like she did until three months ago."

As I listened to Burt tell me about Lannie he said, "When I felt lonely or scared, I could come over to her house. No matter what she was doing Big Granny would stop, make us a cup of honey-sweetened tea and listen. Sometimes the things I talked about were trivial (but at the time they didn't seem that way). She was the one I asked about kissing my first girlfriend and she told me what kind of flowers to buy for the prom. But more than that, she was my role model for just caring about people—about me. From Big Granny, I realized that people are important. 'If you have friends,' she used to say, 'are willing to help others, and believe in God, you really have everything you need.' That's the attitude I want to adopt."

> " 'If you have friends,' she used to say, 'are willing to help others, and believe in God, you really have everything you need.' That's the attitude I want to adopt."

That's the principle of paying back.

I sometimes like to think of paying back as meaning just that: I pay back for all the good things in my life. I can't ever repay God, of course, but I can show my appreciation to God by passing on to those who are walking behind me.

Who Decides
When I'm Old?

I feel so old." I wonder how many times I've heard
that expression. The first time I'm aware of hearing those words, I was sixteen years old. I did hard
manual labor one summer and my coworker complained that way. He was twenty-seven years old. At the
time I wondered if that's what it would feel like to be
twenty-seven.

I heard so much negativity about getting old. As I
wrote when I started this book, for many people it's
easier to deny aging than to face it.

But what would it be like if we considered—and
taught—that aging is a necessary part of the human
condition and part of God's plan for us? Getting older

then becomes our opportunity for spiritual development, and we also point the way for those who are following behind us.

Aging ends in dying. We all know that. Consequently, many of us have made aging the enemy and the steps toward death become battles we must fight. Dylan Thomas screamed out, "Do not go gentle into that good night / Old age should burn and rave at close of day; / Rage, rage against the dying of the light."[10]

How would we regard aging if we could separate it from death? That is, would we more readily accept getting older if we considered it as just one more step—one final step—toward maturity? Otherwise, if we ask why we're old, we are saying (in effect), "It is because I am becoming dead."

Wasn't the death of Jesus Christ on the cross intended to take away our dread of death? The apostle Paul quotes from Isaiah and writes, " 'Death is swallowed up in victory. O death, where is your victory? O death, where is your sting?' For sin is the sting that results in death . . . How we thank God, who gives us victory

Aging ends in dying. We all know that. Consequently, many of us have made aging the enemy and the steps toward death become battles we must fight.

How would we regard aging if we could separate it from death? That is, would we more readily accept getting older if we considered it as just one more step— one final step— toward maturity?

over sin and death through Jesus Christ our Lord!" (1 Cor. 15:54–57 NLT).

Many reflect the attitude of Dylan Thomas and struggle at every age line or sign of aging. If God planned aging and biology is God's way of working through nature to make us more who we really are intended to be, why do we fight it? The older we get the greater our opportunity to like ourselves and to be comfortable with who we are. We're no longer competing with others for jobs, promotions, and material rewards. We're learning to accept and to love ourselves.

> The older we get the greater our opportunity to like ourselves and to be comfortable with who we are . . . the older I become, the more I have to offer others.

As I've pointed out elsewhere, I'm aware that the older I become, the more I have to offer others. They ask my advice, and I give them what I consider commonsense answers. I'm frequently amazed at their responses to my "wisdom." Part of growing older may be to claim such qualities not only as part of our heritage, but also to see them as the gifts we offer others who are behind us on the journey.

As well as getting on in years, are we getting on in becoming what God plans for us to be? Is it possible that the aging process is to strengthen our inner being, to make us more godly?

Isn't it interesting that when people die young, we say, "He died too early," or we speak of "her premature death"? Isn't it remarkable that when we do something soft and generous or cry, we tend to say, "I must be getting soft in my old age," or we make bitter remarks and say that it's only typical of getting older?

Why do we make such statements? Why do we make aging and death negative? Maybe it's because we don't want people to call us old.

Maybe it's because we need to let the right person decide when we're old.

Who decides when I'm old? The correct answer is *I do.*

Too many of us forfeit that right to choose and allow others to label us old. For example, we can consider the idea of mandatory retirement. I'm an ordained minister and my denomination says ministers must retire at age sixty-five. They may stay with their current congregation for an additional five years—but the congregation must vote on them each year for one additional year of service.

> As well as getting on in years, are we getting on in becoming what God plans for us to be? Is it possible that the aging process is to strengthen our inner being, to make us more godly?

Sixty-five has been the business norm for retirement. From its inception in 1935 until the recent change in laws, that's the same age when "old" people can draw full benefits from their retirement.

Ever wonder how we decided that sixty-five is old? To understand, we go back to a misunderstanding of Psalm 91:10: "Seventy years are given to us! Some may even reach eighty. But even the best of these years are filled with pain and trouble" (NLT).

The writer wasn't declaring that people were to die at seventy and a few might hang on for another decade. He was, however, describing in poetic form what he had observed.

Over the centuries, many Christians quoted the verse to mean that God has given us seventy years and a few people struggle on for a few more years.

In Germany in 1899, Prince Otto von Bismark set up the world's first state system of social security. He and his advisers took Psalm 91:10 literally. They subtracted five years from seventy. They reasoned that once people passed their sixty-ninth birthday, they would die soon. They wanted them to benefit from their years of labor and enjoy the last five years of life. So they retired them from the work world.

> *Who decides when I'm old?*
> *The correct answer is I do.*
> *Too many of us forfeit that right to choose and allow others to label us old.*

In the United States, during the presidency of Franklin D. Roosevelt, and following the principle set up in Germany, Congress enacted a law that declared sixty-five as the retirement age.

This means that society has long accepted that retirement means people are too elderly to be productive. It's the age when they die. That misconception is changing. The arbitrary figure implied that people of that age had lost their ability to be productive members of society. Therefore, they left the workplace. By logical application, this says they are too old to be productive.

For the past decade, we've seen a larger number of older Americans who have stayed in the workplace or have become involved in volunteer work. Many of them aren't tucking themselves away in nursing homes or burying themselves in senility. They're active, alive, and making their voices heard.

Americans used to think of work as a job we perform nonstop from our twenties until we retired or died. In earlier generations, that usually meant working for the same company all those years.

We now expand and enlarge our abilities. In the early years of our careers, many claim they haven't reached their peak until their late forties or early fifties. Then they start slowly winding down. But is it possible that some won't hit their peak until their sixties or even their seventies? Some elders will hit their career stride for the first time at an age when others are retiring.

> Society has long accepted that retirement means people are too elderly to be productive. It's the age when they die. That misconception is changing.

If age is an attitude more than a recorded figure in a statistical report, what does that say about our choices? How do we pile up numbers of years lived and yet remain alive and excited about life?

"Throughout my life I have been privileged to know people of great inner strength and character," writes Samantha Landy. "My aunt Bertha lived to be 102. She homesteaded in the Dakotas and chose to laugh in the most arduous circumstances. My aunt Violet is in her nineties and has such great joy too; everyone loves to be with her.

"My secretary, Dorree, is still bright, articulate, and walks daily in the joy of the Lord. She is eighty-two and drives her friends to concerts and dinners because they are afraid to drive at night; even though they are younger than she is.

> I can choose to stay alive and to enjoy every day of my life.

"Our attitude is the most important aspect of the quality of our life, as we become seniors, dealing with the various aspects of aging and with circumstances we cannot control. Our attitude determines how we define our very existence."

So who decides when I'm old?

Ultimately, it's a decision I make.

Will we let events beyond our control overwhelm us or will we look to God to walk with us through each difficulty? It is our choice.

I can choose to stay alive and to enjoy every day of my life. It's a choice.

I've decided to age positively and enjoy the journey.

Facing Death

I'm not afraid to die.

I'm not afraid of the process of dying—although I think of it occasionally. According to polls I've read, most people are more afraid of the act of dying than they are of death itself. They don't want to suffer or be a mental vegetable. And yes, to some extent, that's also true of me. I wonder if I'll die of a lingering illness, a quick death such as a heart attack, or an automobile accident. Yes, I wonder, although that doesn't trouble me deeply.

I do have one lingering fear: *I'm afraid of not being.* Perhaps fear is too strong. Maybe it's better to say I push away thoughts of death. I don't want to ponder or consider what it will be like not to exist.

I have no way of knowing what it's like not to exist. My mind refuses to make sense of a world in which I'm not a participant. Even when I only read or hear about others' experiences, I'm still aware of such things through my senses.

If I'm dead, I have no awareness. What does that mean?

This reluctance isn't a question or dread about my eternal state. My faith enables me to know that I will have a glorious life with Jesus Christ up ahead. I'm not sure if I shoot straight into the presence of God as it is usually taught, following the Greek concept of the immortal soul. The other theological concept is that we have no consciousness in the grave and won't until the resurrection. It doesn't matter which one is correct. Our next conscious moment will be with Jesus Christ. What does matter is that the Bible assures me I'll die and the next waking moment I'll stand in the presence of my Savior.

> I'm not afraid to die. I'm afraid of not being. If I'm dead, I have no awareness.

No, it's not my eternal state that troubles me.

It's the fear of my lack of being.

When I say I'm afraid of *not being,* I mean this life and my senses are all I have. I've spent my life being involved in my world and with other people.

Of course they can cope without me. I just don't want to be left out. I enjoy life too much, and I don't want to miss anything. Even if believers can and do peer down from heaven and see what's going on, that's not the same. I won't be a living participant, and I've never been a good spectator. I want vital participation in the action.

That's part of the reluctance to face death: I know the world will continue to go on. Family members will miss me. Those close to me will shed a number of tears, and a few friends will remember me with a sigh or a quiet sadness, but they'll go on as well.

> When I say I'm afraid of *not being*, I mean this life and my senses are all I have. I've spent my life being involved in my world and with other people.

Maybe that's why *not being* troubles me. It's like walking along the beach at low tide. My feet sink deeply into the wet, sticky sand. I can turn around and see my footprints for three hundred feet behind me. I also know that within hours the tide will return. When the waves cascade over the sand, they will erase all evidence of my presence.

Maybe within each of us resides the desire to make a lasting difference. We can stare at the works of the great artists, or quote stirring poetry, or reread books that are centuries old. We know that although George Frideric Handel has been dead since 1759, our hearts throb when we stand for the "Hallelujah Chorus." More than three hundred years ago, John Bunyan wrote *The Pilgrim's Progress,* but that allegory still speaks to us today. C. S. Lewis died in 1963, but new readers discover his books every year.

Most of us, however, won't be among those names passed on from generation to generation. The most we can expect is to be listed in a great-great-great-grandchild's genealogical research.

Whenever I've imagined my funeral, I've assumed a mourner will say to another, "He used to write a little, didn't he?" I have no idea if my books will endure. The truth is, they probably won't. Even if they endure, I'll never know.

I have taken comfort, however, in acknowledging that I have made a difference now—in this present life.

Perhaps that's where we need to focus our attention— creating an influence that lives on, even if we don't.

For example, occasionally people contact me to tell me how one of my books or an article has influenced them. The day before I wrote my first words for this book, I received a letter postmarked Philadelphia. She didn't send a return address or even her full name. The three-paragraph letter thanked me for giving my words to the world. This was her final sentence: "I'm a better Christian today because of your influence." She signed it *Ann.*

I had made a difference in at least one person's life.

A few years ago I saw a film called *Mr. Holland's Opus.* That film powerfully impacted me and made me think— that's the way I want to influence others.

Mr. Holland, played by Richard Dreyfuss, is a musician who wants to create classical music. To support himself, he takes a job as a high school band director. All the time, however, he constantly dreams of creating his music. He has little time to work on his music because he gives himself to his students. He loves them and heightens their appreciation for music, and he richly influences their lives.

> Perhaps that's where we need to focus our attention—creating an influence that lives on, even if we don't.

At the end of the film, the aged Mr. Holland is forced to

retire, and he feels as if his life has been wasted. He never changed the world with his music. He never created all the wonderful music that floated through his mind.

Unknown to the band director, his wife has contacted people he had taught during his lengthy tenure and asked them to come back as a surprise. In the final scene, they play Mr. Holland's music.

We, the audience, understand. Mr. Holland's opus wasn't the music he wrote; it was the music he wrote in the hearts of his students.

Not everyone can be Mr. Holland or have the opportunity to influence hundreds of lives. Despite our limitations of ability and opportunity, maybe that's the reward we need to receive—the assurance that our lives have made a difference.

> Despite our limitations of ability and opportunity, maybe that's the reward we need to receive— the assurance that our lives have made a difference.

We want to see that difference, not just in books we've written, pictures we've painted, lectures we've given, or sales we've made, we want to make a difference through those we have influenced. Perhaps the most that we can dream of is that we'll influence and encourage a few people.

Consequently, facing the reality of death and our nonexistence is also a way for us to take stock of ourselves. We can ponder how we've used our time, energies, and abilities.

I've concluded that it's not only all right to have anxiety about death, but also that it's normal. Why would I want to leave this life now? I wake up in the mornings, excited that I have today to live.

The more days I have behind me, the fewer I have ahead, but I want to relish every one as it comes to me. My awareness that this will end one day actually makes the present more enjoyable. God gave me these days to appreciate. I'm thankful for every day I wake up and know I'm still on planet Earth.

Notes

1. As quoted in *No Wrinkles on the Soul* by Richard L. Morgan (Upper Room Books, 1990), 38.

2. Jan Kuzma and Cecil Murphey, *Live 10 Healthy Years Longer* (Nasvhille: Word Books, 2000).

3. Kierkegaard made this or similar statements in many of his writings. This is from *Philosophical Fragments,* 80. [public domain]

4. *Time,* November 24, 2003, 49.

5. As quoted in *No Wrinkles on the Soul* by Richard L. Morgan (Upper Room Books, 1990), 38.

6. Charles Dickens, *Great Expectations* (New York: Doubleday, 1997), 99.

7. Ibid., 100.

8. Norman D. Vaughan with Cecil Murphey, *With Byrd at the Bottom of the World* (Mechanicsburg, PA: Stackpole Books, 1990).

9. Cecil Murphey, *The God Who Pursues: Encountering a Relentless God* (Minneapolis: Bethany House, 2002), 25–29.

10. Dylan Thomas, "Do Not Go Gentle into That Good Night." Copyright © 1952, 1953 Dylan Thomas. Copyright © 1937, 1945, 1955, 1962, 1966, 1967 the Trustees for the Copyrights of Dylan Thomas.

You may contact Cec Murphey at
cec_haraka@msn.com or visit his website at
http://cecmurphey.com

If you wish to contact Cec for publicity purposes,
you may contact his publicist, Don Otis at
CMResource@aol.com